Santo[illegible]i
today

**A complete tourist guide...
with 128 colour illustrations
and maps**

TOUBI'S ®

MICHALIS TOUMBIS EDITIONS - ATHENS

Texts: G.I. ALEXAKIS
Translation: G. COX, J. SOLMAN
Maps: NORA ANASTASOGLOU
Photographs: G. YIANNELOS, B. DROSOS, G. KOUMOUROS, K. MANTHOS, M. PETROPOULOS, M. TOUMBIS.

Four-colour editing: YANNIS KOLLAROS
Artwork: NORA ANASTASOGLOU
Photosetting: KIKI SANTORINAIOU
Montage: DIMITRIS SERETIS
Printed by: M. TOUMBIS GRAPHIC ARTS SA, Athens - Tel. no. 9923874

to Santorini
and its people

You emerged from the bowels of the thunder
Shuddering amongst the repenting clouds
Bitter rock, sorely tried and unyielding
You called upon the sun as protomartyr
To face together the hazardous glory
And fare forth upon the ocean, a cross upon your back.

Odysseas Elytis: Ode to Santorini

Publisher's Foreword

Santorini is not just an island; it has not developed as its island neighbours have. Its history, together with its people and their works, has been buried in the ground and born again more than once! It is for that reason that Santorini is unlike any other island! It is quite different and alone and it lives in its own way. Even its people are different; they say of themselves... "We' re not people — we' re Santorinians".

For that reason, too, it is impossible to describe Santorini in an ordinary way. In order to describe it you have to embark on a search —a lengthy search— during the course of which you will come to love and believe in the island. In order to convey the sense of 'differentness' about this island, you have to commune with the richness, history and geological sensitivity of the landscape. This is where we, in publishing this book, and you, in reading it, have been fortunate.

It should be borne in mind that not all of the author's achievements are contained in the book in your hand. The nature of this edition compelled us to omit some details which would have been better suited to a study of the island's folklore and nothing else. The compilation of the book, its enhancement with appropriate photographic material and its harmonious presentation have been a difficult and painstaking task.

The publisher

Contents

Introduction

I wonder what impression Santorini makes on someone seeing it for the first time.

I no longer remember what my first impression was —I was very small when first taken to the island— but I do remember being pleased with the sight of its reddish-black earth. I would sit by the hour just gazing at its precipices, the huge scarred masses of stone which tower out of the sea, its black stones with their surfaces shiny as steel. And when I was sent on errands to the market, I gladly stopped whatever game I might be playing simply because I knew that on the way I would be able to slip into someone else's yard, which would have a view different to that to be gained from ours. I would have been about seven then. Later, at school, they taught me the words "grandeur" and "imposing", and I knew at once what they meant. What they were telling us about was Skaros, Apano Meria, Droumbes. Many years were to pass before I saw anywhere else which brought to mind the words "grandeur" and "imposing" — until I saw Mount Taygetus, in fact. And that, I think, will be the end of that.

Anyone who visits Santorini for the first time with some experience of other Greek islands is certainly going to be somewhat taken aback. Santorini is a strange island, without any similarity to the rest of the Cyclades. They, taken as a whole, I think of as musical variations on the same theme. They give you a sense of harmony, calm, relaxation. All the lines, colours, sounds and styles are gentle. The other islands feel friendly, warm and tender as an embrace; Santorini is neither calm nor gentle. On the contrary, it is wild and threatening; its patterns and colours are harsh. It thrusts up out of the sea like a gigantic chiaroscuro by Goya.

The whole island is one huge pile of volcanic lava. The ground you stand on is not part of the earth's crust; it has been created by the hardening of a viscous liquid expelled from the bowels of the earth, like the blood from a wound drying on the skin. Red, black and brown are its colours. The history of Santorini is punctuated by the upheavals of creation and by catastrophes of epic magnitude. At one stage half the island broke away and was sucked down into the depths, so that the Santorini that you see today is no more than a relic of the other Santorini, the complete one. Every so often earthquakes shake the island and there is no knowing if everything will stay in its place. In the parts that are lived in the majority of the houses are ruins gaping to the sky. The sea around it is 380 metres deep — and it is deepest dark blue right to the water's edge. For a ship to drop anchor is out of the question. A French traveller who, two centuries ago, drew a map of the island, marked the sea with the nightmare indication "bottomless". Around Santorini it is only the sea which separates you from the abyss, and in its midst floats the volcano — swarthy and lean like a crocodile's back.

In the face of all this, awe is the natural reaction. But this awe is precisely the most valuable thing that Santorini has to offer. In time one gets over the grandeur, the picturesqueness, even the fear: but the awe remains. This is because you know that what is revealed before you are the bowels of the earth, the mother of us all, and that here, with confidence and without shame, you can lay down all the myths you carry with you.

The island is a huge heap of volcanic lava. (Oia).

Santorini and its volcano; "The Illustrate

ondon News", March 31 1866, p. 318

THE HISTORY OF SANTORINI

The history of Santorini in not just human history. It is the history of a place which has the unlikely distinction of evolving and taking shape of itself and which does so constantly, even today. In order to grasp this, try to think back to an Aegean with the Cyclades but without Santorini. Then imagine the island one day rising from the sea's depths, gaining height, drying out and eventually being peopled as the home of a major culture. Next picture another day, on which half the island founders, taking its people and their achievements with it under the ashes and the waves. When the turmoil dies down, new inhabitants come to the island, give it a name of their own and start again from scratch. And now imagine another island rising from the sea bit by bit and taking the place of the one which sank... The history of Santorini is the history of a place which is not to be taken for granted and whose map must from time to time be scrapped and re-drawn all over again.

Even today we are not in a position to know with complete accuracy and total certainty all Santorini's geological ups and downs. There is no shortage of theories, hypotheses and interpretations, and though these may appear to conflict they converge at the salient points in helping one to form a fairly clear picture of the various phases in the process of parturition which brought "devil's island" into the world. In a history stretching back so many millions of years it hardly matters if one is a thousand or two thousand years out.

The island's geological history begins at a time when Europe and Africa were still joined. At that time, what is today the Aegean was dry land (Aegeis) and it linked mainland Greece with Asia Minor and Crete. After a long series of geological upheavals, Aegeis sank beneath the surface of the waves. This must have happened about six million years ago. The mountain peaks of the 'lost continent' protruded above the water and are what we call today the islands of the Aegean Sea. The position occupied today by Santorini had to show only two or three insignificant islets, which are still there today, in

Map of Santorini: M. Boschini, Venice, 1654.

Map of Santorini: T. Porcacchi, Venice, 1572.

Map of Santorini: G.F. Camocio, Venice, 1571-5

In 2000 BC the inhabitants of Strongyle knew how to build two-storey houses; they were sensitive to colours and skilled artist.

corporated into the principal island. They are the mountain known as Prophitis Ilias, the Athinios rocks above the modern harbour, and Monolithos, an isolated obtruding rock on the east coast of the island. They are easy to recognise if one looks at their rock formation, which is strikingly different to that of the rest of the island. At that time, of course, there was no volcano.

The volcano first manifested itself 80,000 years or so ago. This first eruption was terrific. Ash found on the sea bed and originating with that eruption covers an area stretching from Chios to Italy, North Africa and almost as far as Cyprus. Before this ash settled on the sea bed it must have darkened the skies over that area for a very long time. Apart from the ash, the crater expelled other, heavier, substances which poured forth in liquid or semi-liquid form at great heat and formed a cone. The cone gradually grew, covering the surface of the sea and joining with the islets which were already there to form an approximately circular island with a diameter of 14 to 15 kilometres.

We do not know how many centuries passed before this island took its final form. What we do know is that about 2000 BC (that is, the time at which Minoan civilization was reaching its peak in Crete), the island was inhabited by people who called it Strongyle ('round'). These people had the art of building two-storey houses, of tilling the earth and of producing olive oil and wheat; they had domesticated sheep, from whose milk they made cheese, they fished, they wove, and they decorated their pottery, their houses and themselves. They were very sensitive to colour, and were capable of producing wonderful paintings. In order to get a concrete picture of the life these people led, all the visitor need do is go to the site of the recent archaeological dig at Akrotiri, where a complete town, dating from this period, has been discovered under the ash (See route Fira-Akrotiri, p. 115).

The volcano erupted for a second time, equally destructively, in a much more recent epoch, c. 1450 BC. The eruption wiped out all life on the island. It would appear that directly beneath the centre of Strongyle the outpouring of lava during the eruption created an enormus hollow 'dome' which, in the end, was unequal to supporting the weight of the island. The roof of the 'dome' fell in, and with it the greater part of Strongyle sank beneath the waves which rushed in to cover it. All that was left above the surface of the sea were segments of its perimeter, which extend, like open arms, around the gigantic sea basin, known in vulcanological terms as the caldera. It is these arms which today are called Santorini, Thirasia and Aspronisi. If one thinks of the panic and fear generated in any of us by the slightest earth tremor, just because the earth shakes a little beneath our feet, or because the light hanging from the ceiling swings to and fro a little, it may be possible to conceive the extent and the horror of this fearful eruption. Eighty four square kilometres of solid ground collapsed to the bed of the sea, with a crash which it must have been possible to hear in Norway. The sky over the Aegean was covered by an enormous black cloud of smoke and ash and a tidal wave 250 metres high rushed outwards at a speed of 350 kilometres per hour. In less than half an hour it had reached Crete and drowned the

13 Diagram of the Mediterranean showing the extent of the eruption.

whole of Minoan civilization.

These events, though proved beyond any doubt to have occurred, are, nonetheless, not mentioned, even as a memory, in any of the texts of antiquity. It is only in the ancient Greek myths and in the symbolism of the Old Testament that one encounters the echo of terrible disturbances of nature in the Mediterranean fourteen or fifteen centuries before the birth of Christ, disturbances which must, at least as a hypothesis, be connected with the eruption of Santorini in about 1450. The myth of Deucalion and Pyrrha, for instance, who were the sole survivors of the flood sent by Zeus to punish mankind, may well directly reflect the eruption of Santorini. This flood can be placed chronologically some where between 1530 and 1400 BC*. Another flood myth is that concerning Poseidon, who in anger gave Attica up to the waters when he lost the contest with Athena over which of them was to be sovereign in Athens. The death of Hippolytus, too, was the result of a giant wave raised by Poseidon — again — near Troezen. To give a last instance, the myths say that ten or fifteen years, at most, before the death of Hippolytus Theseus had relieved the Athenians of their tribute to Crete. Could the truth of the matter really be that the state of Minos no longer existed?

Turning to the Old Testament, it is not an unfeasible hypothesis that the plagues of Egypt were among the more far-reaching consequences. To quote Kontaratos:** *"The land of the Pharaohs must have been overwhelmed with oxides of iron, which turned water red, compounds of sulphur, which poison all life, and flaming volcanic ash, which burned up all vegetation, and it must have been inundated by an all-consuming flood"*. How can one fail to find this convincing when we know from eyewitness reports that later eruptions, incomparably less powerful than that of 1450 BC, produced the same phenomena in Santorini? (See below, p. 20).

However things may be, total destruction was succeeded by the return of calm once more. Hesitantly at first, people and then the volcano began to resume their normal routine. All we know of the first settlers to dare to land on the island is what can be concluded from the myths. It would seem to have been the Phoenicians who were first drawn by the beauty of the landscape, around 1300 BC. They colonised the island and gave it a new name, Calliste ("the most beautiful" in Greek). Towards the end of the 12th century BC, and possibly in 1115, more colonists arrived: Dorians from Sparta, under their king Theras, son of Autesion and great-great-grandson of Oedipus. The island changed its name once more, and harbours, cities and temples rose. In 825 BC, the Phoenician alphabet was introduced to Thera. In 630 a long period of drought induced the desperate islanders to send out an expedition which colonised Cyrene, on the north coast of Africa. Later, we find the island as an ally of the Spartans, and still later as tributary to Athens. In the Hellenistic period it was a naval base for the Ptolemies of Egypt. The ancient city of Thera, at Mesa Vouno (see the Fira-Kamari-Mesa Vouno

*This fact and many others are given by A.N. KONTARATOS in his detailed and lucid "Review of the Prehistory of Santorini", Athens, 1970.

** op., cit., p. 49

route, p. 102, for more details) dates from this time. Both the overlordship of the Ptolemies and the importance of Santorini as a base ended with the coming of the Romans.

The Byzantine church of Our Lady Episkopi Gonia (detail).

Santorini was converted to Christianity in the 3rd century, and became the see of a bishop, the first incumbent being Dioscurus (342-344). Under Justinian the see of Santorini and eleven others were placed under the administration of Rhodes. The most worthwhile Byzantine monument to have survived is the elegant little church of Our Lady 'Episkopi Gonia', built by the Emperor Alexios I Comnenus (1081-1118) on early Christian ruins (see the Fira-Kamari-Mesa Vouno route, p. 98).

The 'Franks', as the Crusaders and their offshoots were called in medieval Greece, arrived in 1204. Their capital was the Skaros fortress, and their arrival was the start of a new period of trials and tribulations for the islanders. There were disputes between the Dukes of Naxos and of Santorini (the name dates from this period), attempts on the part of the Byzantine Empire to liberate the island, Turkish raids, outbursts of murderous jealousy between Genoa and the Serene Republic of Venice, but it was the islanders who footed the bill no matter who might be fighting whom. Only on one occasion did the island change hands peacably — in 1480, when the Duke of Santorini gave it as dowry to his daughter, who was marrying the Duke of Crete. Even that did not last long, for the bride's uncle disagreed, and when he came to power he withdrew the grant of dowry.

Ancient Thera as the site is today.

Life did become a little quieter when Santorini became part of the Ottoman Empire, in 1579. However, so many centuries of internal turmoil — quite apart from the damage done by the raids of corsairs — had decimated the population. It is unlikely that there were more than five hundred inhabitants at that time. The Turks did not colonise the island.

A view of Oia: drawing by J.B. Hilaire.

They were, however, impressed by its windmills and called Santorini 'Deyrmetcik' -'Little Mill'. In all other respects the island retained relative autonomy; the inhabitants themselves elected their headmen, who represented them before the Ottoman authorities. The Catholics, with their bishop, lived at Skaros, while the Orthodox in the other fortresses and villages had a bishop of their own. As piracy gradually died out, the island began to recover, to engage in trade and to acquire its own fleet. In 1821 the fleet of Santorini was the third largest in Greece, after those of Hydra and Spetses, with 5,000 tons. By 1852 Santorini had fallen back to fifth place, although its fleet had doubled in size. At this date Syros, Spetses, Galaxidi and Hydra had larger fleets. After Santorini came Piraeus, in sixth place.

The records of foreign travellers form a rich source of information on the years of Turkish rule. In a

Engraving of Skaros by Thomas Hope (1769-1831).

Skaros today.

Dress of the women of Santorini; lithograph, Paris, 1843.

Male and female costume of Santorini; drawing by J. Grosset.

Male costume of Santorini; engraving by J. Laroque.

Female costume of Santorini; engraving by J. Grosset de Saint Souveur.

Chronicle which he published in Paris in 1657, French Jesuit Francois Richard gives a vivid picture of the inhabited parts of the island in the mid-17th century:

"In Santorini there are five towns or fortified places (pyrgi). The first is called Kastro, and enjoys the respect of all. It was there that the Dukes and Governors of the island lived before it became subject to the Turks. It was also the site of the ducal palace. Today Kastro is the seat of the Latin bishop.*

"Kastro stands at a great height and it takes half an hour to reach its walls. Its gates used to be closed when an enemy attack was feared or corsairs landed. There used to be two hundred houses on the cliff which rises in its very centre. These have now been abandoned and little by little are being pulled down. No one now has any wish to live at such a height. It was with the stones of the ruined houses that we built our church.

"It is said that at the top of the cliff there used to be a great bell to warn the people whenever a corsair ship appeared at sea. At the present time when danger threatens they light beacons as they do in the other islands.

"The name of the second fortress is Pyrgos. It stood in the middle of its little town and was used by the inhabitants as a place of refuge in wartime. This is where the cadi who came to island every two years to administer justice used to stay. But since the outbreak of the Cretan War between Turkey and the Venetians the latter, having control of the sea, have held hostage all the Turks of the Aegean islands and permit no new Ottoman settlements.

"Nowadays the island is governed by the headmen, who must pay tax both to the Sultan and to the Serene Republic of Venice.

"The third fortified place is called Emborio, that is to say, Market. This is where the sale of all merchandise takes place.

"The other two fortresses are situated at the two extremes of the islands: one at Apanomeria and the other at Akrotiri.

*"There are also many villages: Karterados, Messaria, Megalo Chorio, and others. Karterados apart from the Greeks, has two hundred Catholics**".*

Alongside the human life of the island, the volcano continued to have a life of its own. Various craters in the centre of the caldera erupted from time to time — these of course were totally insignificant in comparison with the previous one; but they did begin again the process of filling in the caldera. The lava formed cone-shaped accretions, under the sea initially, around the craters. These later projected above the surface of the sea and have made up — for the present — in many successive phases the two islands Palaia and Nea Kameni, which are today simply called "The Volcano". There were fourteen such eruptions of the Volcano between 198 BC and 1950:

* He is referring to Skaros.

** This text, and many others descriptive of Greece, can be found (in Greek) in Kyriakos Simopoulos, "Foreign Travellers in Greece", Athens, 1972.

TABLE OF DATES OF ERUPTIONS

Number of eruption	Date	Interval between this and previous eruption	Changes in the form of the island
1	198-6 BC.		
2	19 AD.	215 years	Palaia or Megali Kameni formed in successive phases (Mikri Kameni was formed in 1573).
3	60	41 years	
4	726	666 years	
5	1457	731 years	
6	1508	51 years	
7	1573	65 years	Mikri Kameni, later to be incorporated into Nea Kameni, formed.
8	1650	77 years	Outside the caldera, in the sea to the NE of the island. No obvious change.
9	1707-12	57 years	The various fragments which gradually united to form the present-day Nea Kameni — the main bulk of the volcano — made successive apearances.
10	1866-70	154 years	
11	1925-26	55 years	
12	1928	2 years	
13	1940-41	12 years	
14	1950	9 years	Small successive eruptions.

The volcano erupts; engraving, 1866.

The eruption of 1650, which took place outside the caldera at a distance of 6.5 km from the north-eastern coast of Santorini, at a spot called Koloumbos, is described by the Jesuit Francois Richard in his Chronicle. The cone formed round this crater did not protrude above the surface of the sea. It still exists today, in the form of a reef at a depth of 18.5 metres.

"On the night of 27th September a new and more terrible earthquake made the houses reel hither and thither like babies' cradles and shook them like reeds in the wind.

"After this tremor we saw four miles to the east, between Andros and Santorini, flames wrapped in dense clouds leaping from the sea. A pall of smoke rose on high from the blazing abyss. Then the fiery clouds lowered upon us, with a fearsome stench, as if as the flames were coming from Hell itself.

"Six days before we had observed that the sea in that area was bright green in colour, a clear sign that the fire lurking in the depths was struggling to force open a cleft in the sea-bed and that sulphurous fumes were escaping into the water.

"In the two days which followed the flaring up of the flames the ocean burned with an ever-increasing vigour, the earth tremors redoubled, the smoke grew ever thicker and the surface of the sea became covered with the pumice disgorged by the abyss.

"Notwithstanding this, our fear was nothing to what it was to become on Sunday, 29 September. This was the most terrible day of which history can speak. The sea growled menacingly, the earth quivered and the very air was afire. Thick sulphurous steam billowed out of the depths and rose on high as black clouds. Then suddenly the clouds caught fire, lightning rent the sky, thunder burst forth and strange forms moved before one's eyes: flying snakes, shining spears and lances and whirling blazing torches.

"All that day the clouds hung low, the island shook and the wild elements met in such raging combat that their clamour could be heard a hundred leagues off. Ash fell as far away as Asia Minor. At Palatia it covered the grapes on the unharvested vine. The ash was like white chalk or burned gypsum. The Turks said the islands were no more; fire from heaven had smitten them.

"It was observed by many that as the great peal of thunder rang out, the subterranean fire cast up into the heavens enormous rocks, which fell to earth again two leagues away. In a field we saw a boulder spewed from the bowels of the earth, of a size that 40 men together could not move it.

"Many of the islanders went stone blind for two or three days together. Their eyes geve them dire pain, they shrieked both day and night. Fifty souls and some thousand beasts were lost in this fell visitation, suffocated by the poisonous vapours.

"All the gold and silver objects enclosed within pouches or chests and all the gilt and silvered things and embroideries turned black. The sacred vessels in the churches were altered in appearance, although they had been covered in their veils. Those icons which were unvarnished looked as if they had been totally obliterated, but the colours revived when washed with wine and vinegar. The silver objects, too, regained their lustre when

burnished with oil and warm ash.

*"Nine poor sailors, returning from Amorgos, their boats laden with wheat, came too close to the brim of the flaming chasm and were lost. Their charred bodies were found after three days and their boats drifted upon the sea with no hand on the tiller"**.*

Fifty seven years later, in 1707, activity began in the centre of the caldera once more, being accompanied this time by the disturbing phenomenon of islands appearing where previously there had been only sea. These eruptions were observed by Tarillon, another Jesuit, who happened to be in Santorini that year:

*"... On 18 May two minor earth tremors were experienced on the island. No one, however, paid any heed. It would appear that at that moment the islet began to rise up from the depths of the sea and to break through the surface of the waters. Whatever the truth of the matter may be, the sailors, seeing that morning the topmost points of the islet emerging, assumed that what they were seeing were the remains of a shipwreck that had taken place the previous night. They thus embarked in their boats and hastened to the spot to salvage what they might from the 'ship'. However, it was not a ship they encountered, but rocks. The islanders in fear returned as fast as they might to port and told others of the strange sight that they had seen"***.*

Three days later, some of the bolder islanders approached the new islet in their boats and landed on it. But then...

"They suddenly felt the rocks begin to move and the ground upon which they were standing tremble. Dismayed, they abandoned the islet and made for their boats. This tremor was no more than a slight movement of the island as it grew. Within a few days it was twelve metres across and six metres high.

"Nonetheless, the island grew neither regularly nor in proportion. Many a time it would sink back at one point while swelling and spreading at another. One day a huge rock emerged from the very middle of the reef and rose to a height of some 15 metres. I observed it carefully for four days. Suddenly it sank once more into the sea and was lost to view. There were rocks, too, which would sink for a few days, appearing and disappearing beneath the surface of the waters, and in the end locked themselves into place. All these perturbations shook Mikri Kameni to its roots, and for the first time a deep crack appeared in its summit.

"In the meantime the sea in the bay had been changing colour ceaselessly: from bright green to reddish and then to a light yellow. An oppressive odour rose from the depths of the water.

"Smoke was seen emerging from the new islet for the first time on 16 July. Not from that portion of it which was visible, however — it came from a chain of black rocks which had emerged at a point where the sea until then had been bot-

* op. cit., A, pp. 534-5

** op. cit., B, pp. 53

tomless. These rocks formed two separate islands, one of which was named Aspronisi ('white island') and the other Mavronisi ('black island') owing to their colour. A little later, however, the two islets joined together, with the black rocks at their centre. Thick whitish smoke poured forth incessantly.

"On the night of 19 to 20 July, flames were seen to spring from the midst of this smoke. The islanders of Skaros were seized with panic. Their houses stood but half a league away and the castle hung dizzily over precipices which fell sheer into the sea. They expected that at any moment the fire, which must surely be creeping into the bowels of their own rock, would make an end of them. They decided to abandon the fortress and make with their belongings for another island or for another corner of Santorini.

"The Turks who chanced to be in the island to collect the taxes were overcome with fear. Beside themselves at the spectacle of the fire rising from the abyss, they exhorted the people to offer up prayers to God and urged the children to run out into the streets and cry 'Lord, have mercy on us'. For, as they held, the innocent children, not yet having blasphemed against God as had their elders, retained their purity, and might, by their prayers, appease the divine wrath.

"Nonetheless, the fire was not as yet worthy of mention, springing as it did from only one spot on Mavronisi and not being visible at all during the day.

"Aspronisi seemed quiet: neither smoke nor fire. The other, however, grew constantly. Each day huge boulders could be seen coming to the surface; the island grew wider and narrower by turns and the boulders sometimes merged with the main body of the island and sometimes drew away from it. Before a month was out there were four 'mavronisia', which then suddenly united into one single mass.

"The smoke grew thicker and thicker and as the weather was windless it rose so high that it could be seen from Crete, Naxos and other distant islands. There was a pillar of fire by night and on the sea floated a foam which was reddish in some places and yellowish in others. Then the clouds of smoke drifted so as to cover the whole of Santorini. The islanders felt themselves suffocating and struggling for breath, and to keep down the fearful stench they burned incense and lit fires in the streets. However, this lasted only two days. A strong sirocco sprang up and dispersed the smoke, which, however, in the meantime, had passed over the vineyards and scorched the ripening grapes. Silver and copperware changed colour and tarnished. The people suffered from migraines and vomiting. The white island suddenly fell some three metres.

"On 31 July the sea began to seethe at two circular spots, nine and eighteen metres from the black island. At these points the water burned like oil on a fire. The boiling lasted a month, and dead fish were washed up on the shore day and night.

"On 1 August a deep reverberating booming sound was heard, as if many cannons were being fired together afar off. A little later two flames sprang from the submarine furnace, soared high into the air and extinguished themselves.

"On 17 August the islet began to spout jets of flame and the sea around it gave off smoke and boiled with foam. Fire poured from 60 or more orifices. The sea continued to be covered with that reddish foam which stank fearfully.

"Every night after the hollow roaring to which we had become accustomed lambent tongues of fire could be seen springing from the sea's depths, with millions of lights which shot up into the heavens and then fell back like a rain of stars upon the island, itself all aglow. As the fire disported itself, another strange phenomenon took its turn to strike awe into the islanders. Amidst the flames winging through the air, one tongue of fire detached itself and hung high and attenuated for some time over the fortress of Skaros. As the hearts of the islanders rose into their mouths at this evil omen, the tongue of fire sprang still higher and was lost among the clouds.

"On 9 September the two islands joined to become one solid mass. Only four of their 60 craters continued to vomit fire. Smoke and flames were belched forth from these openings, sometimes with thunderous noises and sometime with wild whistling sounds, reminiscent of the howling of beasts.

"The submarine rumblings died down somewhat after 12 September. All that was heard from time to time was thunder like massed artillery fire. Now and then huge incandescent stones were thrown up out of each crater. The clouds of smoke became whirlwinds and an endless rain of ash fell upon the island.

"The eruptions gained in force once more after 18 September. The boulders emitted from the craters collided with each other in the air with fearful crashes. Then they would fall back, on Santorini or splashing into the sea. Mikri Kameni often seemed completely covered by these incandescent boulders, and glowed in the night.

"On 21 September Mikri Kameni was all alight. Suddenly three thunderbolts lit up the horizon from end to end. The new island was shaken to the depths; it quaked and shuddered from side to side. One of the craters sank and vast boulders were hurled to a distance of three miles. Four days of calm followed before the pandemonium broke loose once more. The explosions were continuous and so loud that two persons shouting to each other face to face were unable to hear what the other said. People hastened in panic to the churches. The Skaros rock could be seen to undulate and the doors of the houses banged open of their own accord.

"The eruptions did not stop at all until February 1708. On 10 February the volcano let loose again. Mountainous rocks were spewed forth from the crater, the island shook, subterranean rumbling filled the heart with fear and the sea boiled. There was an explosion every two minutes. The flames could now be seen by day for the first time.

*"This inferno continued until 23 May. The new island spread and gained height ceaselessly. Lava extended the great crater. Then at last all was calm"**.

What happened in 1956 was not an eruption, but an earthquake — one which wrought fearful havoc on the island.

---

* op. cit., B, pp. 54-57

SANTORINI (THIRA)

N. PALEA KAMENI
GEO
N. ASPRO
TO KRITI
Ormos Athinios
Athinios
Vothonas
Exo Gonia
Pyrgos
Episkopi Gonias
Megalochori
Papagia Gonias
Kamari
PROFITIS ILIAS
Moni Profiti Ilia (Museum)
566
ARCHAIA THIRA
369
Messa Vouno
MESSA VOUNO
Perissa
Moni Zoodochou Pigis
Ormos Perissa
Emporio
DIAPLA
CHIROBILIA
Agios Nikitas
Agia Anna
Ormos Balos
Theoskepasta
LOUMARADES
210
Akrotiri
Akr. Akrotiri
MISSA PIGADIA
Akr. Mavro Vouno
Messa Pigadi
AKROTIRI
Kokkini Ammos
Ormos Akrotiri
GAVRILOS
VLYCHADA
Vlychada
Ormos Vlychada
ELEFSINA
Akr. Exo Mytis
Agios Georgios
PERIVOLOS
Perivolos
Ormos Ai Giorgi
Asphalt Road
Non - Asphalt Road
Road in poor condition
Gave
Airport
Castle
Monastery
Archaeological Site

YESTERDAY AND TODAY

The earthquake did not damage only the buildings. It demolished a whole epoch and buried it for ever. This out-of-the-way, half-forgotten island, southernmost of the Cyclades, was suddenly a name on everyone's lips — front page of the newspapers, first item on the news, the apple of the state's eye, bustling with people and activity. Social security agencies, stretcher-bearers, civil servants, workmen, engineers, architects, building sites, compensation, grants and speculation. At the same time, though —and this is neither the first nor the last peculiar thing about Santorini— the earthquake was responsible for unearthing a considerable proportion of the island's population. At least half the islanders must up to that time have been living out of sight in the diggings known today as 'skafta' and shown off as traditional forms of house. All these people came out on to the surface for once, got a taste of the sun and new houses which were built on top of the ground as opposed to being dug out of it, and gradually came to realise that they were now the owners of ruins which were beginning to acquire considerable value. All in all, what happened was that immediately after the earthquake the locals and the imported talent set about putting the island back on its feet. The first thing needed, of course, was some kind of rudimentary infrastructure. Among the first measures were electrification, the extension of the island's primitive road network and the construction of a new harbour which would be accessible not only to ships but also to wheeled transport on the island. In more recent years the telephone, an airport and, lastly, the cable-car. These innovations brought about earth-shattering changes on the island, but the islanders, accustomed to literally earth-shattering upheavals, reacted with utter calm and a good deal of philosophy: "Earthquake? So what?" And that in turn means that when they started laying new foundations over the ruins of their island they knew, somewhere in the depths of their souls, that they would be building a new era.

It was tourism that gave this new era its character. In the beginning there were some far-sighted foreigners who started to buy up ruins, re-build them —with every respect for the local style of architecture— and use them for their own purposes or as rented properties. These first pioneers were followed by more far-sighted foreigners, and then by more, and more, and more. In the end, of course, the Greeks woke up too, saw that there was money in the business and rolled up their sleeves. In their turn, they began to buy up ruins and rebuild them. White blobs —the rebuilt houses— started to appear here and there against the grey backround of the ruins; in the end, the whole place became white again, with only the occasional grey blob to bear witness to the catastrophe. In the meantime travel to and from the island had become easier, supply difficulties were overcome and the tourists started to arrive. The islanders were initiated into the science of the rented room. After all, a place with so many natural attractions needs very little to turn itself into a magnet for tourists.

And so the question of what the islanders of Santorini do about work today has a self-evident answer: tourism, of course. In the summer the island is swamped by visitors, life

takes place in the open air and the locals work at breakneck speed. When winter comes everything goes dead, the people shut themselves up in their houses and catch up on lost sleep. And in the spring, before the tourists start to arrive, the island is a hive of activity as preparations are made and everything is repainted and freshened up. None of this, however, is of particular interest to us; there is nothing new or extraordinary about it, and, more important, it does not (yet) reflect the real physiognomy of the island. Perhaps if we are to find that we will have to go back into the past a little — not far, just twenty five or thirty years or so. There are quite a few reasons why this is advisible.

First of all, the people who lived through that time, the years before the earthquake, are still to be found. All the islanders of over the age of thirty or so were born and brought up during that period. And when we go to the island, it is these people we will come in contact with, they are the ones whom we will want to get to know and understand. No matter how large the changes of the last thirty years may have been, no matter how grindingly soul-destroying their daily round may be today, there must surely be something left of the individuality of a race whose boast was once "We're not human beings, we're Santorinians". And it is important that we identify what that something may be, for it is that which is formulated by new conditions to provide —if it can, or perhaps it even has already— a new individuality.

Another reason for examining the recent past is to try to understand why it should be that the islanders gave themselves over to tourism body and soul. It is generally accepted that although tourism provides direct financial benefits —and considerable ones, at that— it is also disastrous from the cultural point of view. That view is held at least of tourism as we know it in Greece. This is not the place to go into the rightness or wrongness of the general principle (though it probably is right: look around you). What is of interest to us is that one result of this concept is the constant expression of pious hopes that cultural identity can be maintained, that something will survive. These hopes and wishes are accompanied by nostalgia, disillusion, pessimism, anger and —much more rarely— by activities aimed at getting something done. Let us linger for a moment over the people who express anger and censure the islanders who found themselves a source of easy profit, a goose which really does lay golden eggs, and turned their backs on everything else. Anyone who can make criticisms of this kind must surely be ignorant of what destitution means. Destitution means having nothing, absolutely nothing: no salary, no income, not a day's work here and there or any hope of ever getting any. Matters we associate today with other centuries, or with other continents. The Santorinians had a word for it -δυστυχάμε- expressive not only of misery itself but also of its permanence and limitlessness. The word was indicative of a different order of things among people, an order which included those who had families of twelve, or sixteen, or eighteen children, and who counted themselves fortunate when war came along and carried off half the children, allowing the others to live. Life was no laughing matter, given that even then each household would be left with six, or eight, or nine children. The land, of course, is fruitful, and its produce is top quality, although there is some lack of variety. Some of the staples —flour, potatoes, olive oil, meat— are imported and have to be paid for, and then who owned the fields anyway? And how many hands would be needed to till them? What about the others? The father, a boatman, might get work only one day a week and the boat wasn't his anyway. The mother might work as a cleaner, and would have to wait for the summer for a local living in Athens to come to the island for a couple of months' holiday to earn a wage or two. There might be eight children in the family, until the oldest girl grew up —that is, reached the age of twelve— and could be sent off to Athens to go into service. It was all very like a nineteenth century romantic novel. The servant girl, in her turn, would spend all winter setting aside her pittance so as to be able, 'going down' for the summer, to buy seven pairs of linen shoes for her brothers and sisters. The word 'greedy' can perhaps be used of those whose stomachs are full; it is hardly applicable to the poor.

All this makes the situation today much more understandable. What it does not mean, however, is that the sudden passage from wretchedness to comfort has not been without its price. The nostalgia we were talking about above is not simply a matter of sentiment. It conceals awareness of a very specific danger: that everything will be lost, everything will be forgotten — we shall be left rootless. What is in question is not progress, development and social transformation. That would be ludicrous, for the world has never ceased to evolve. What is in question is memory — the thoughtless despoliation of memory, for memory is of the essence of culture. Why on earth should development be cognate with destruction? Why on earth should we abuse memory —for who can doubt that 'our ancestors the ancient Greeks' are as often as not a straitjacket— while at the same time letting granny sell the family heirlooms to the rag and bone man? There cannot but be a saner way to do things and one day the Greeks too will have to find a right way to cherish memory.

Oia

Most of the islandersused to live in houses hewn out of the earth like hobbit-holes. This way round the housing problem was a consequence of the formation and composition of the ground, of the lack of building materials and the very serious problems encountered in transporting them. If one looks at Santorini from a distance it will be seen that the island seems to consist of masses of land rising more or less vertically out of the sea. There are no slopes, only precipices. The land masses are a ranged perpendicularly, each a little behind the other. The overall appearance is that of land rising in gigantic terraces which are higher than they are deep. Even the back side of the island, which descends more gently towards the sea, descends in terraces. The net result is that perpendicular planes predominate over the horizontal ones. On the other hand, the ground or at least the topsoil consists of a kind of firm whitish sand. The mixture is one of volcanic dust, earth and ash and it has the dual advantage of being easy to dig while being solid enough not to cave in once hollowed out (most of the houses which survived the earthquake were 'skafta'). These two factors combined to provide the islanders with the most simple of solutions: they dug a horizontal tunnel in the ground, built a wall across the mouth and moved in. This expedient had not only the beauty of simplicity but also the force of necessity, for the island has none of the usual building materials: there is no clay for bricks, there are no trees for timber and, most important of all, there is no water. All there is is stones, of a type impossible to work and there is not a trace of the schist rock formations which would allow traditional dry stone techniques to be used.

And so the 'skafta' came into being: long narrow passages with vaulted ceilings. The entry was the only point of access for fresh air and light, and for that reason there were many openings in the wall across it: the door, with its light directly above it, and windows to the right and left of it. The house was divided into two communicating rooms divided by a wall parallel to that across the entrance, of which, in fact, it was an exact copy; it too had a door in the middle with windows above and to the right and left of it, thus admitting light into the further room, which was the bedroom. Sometimes there was a third room, even further in, used as a storeroom. This was called the 'skoteino' ('the dark room'). The front room was the parlour.

To be strictly accurate the above description is somewhat schematic. In reality, the mountain was never exactly vertical and a part of the house would protrude; the tunnel would be built out for a certain distance, but rarely far enough to allow windows to be incorporated into the sides of the extension. In front of each house was a courtyard. This was absolutely essential. Around it stood the tiny kitchen, the privy and perhaps a henhouse or two. All these were Lilliputian stone constructions with vaulted ceilings. The water cistern was dug in the yard, serving to collect rainwater either directly or from the roofs and lead it off into the cistern. The outside of the houses was not usually whitewashed, although the roofs were, to keep the rainwater clean. The fronts of the houses were the colour of their plaster, that is to say, of the earth — a very light, whitish ash colour. The plaster in its turn was decorated with reddish or greyish black pebbles pressed into it at random intervals. This method of decoration is still used today when houses are being restored, although it is all too obvious that it is copied. Even something as simple as this strikes a false note as soon as it stops being spontaneous. Could it be the fault of the large quantities of cement used in mixing plaster? Could a certain degree of symmetry in the placing of pebbles be to blame? However it may be, something tells you that what you are seeing is not authentic.

The houses themselves were not as nighmarish as the idea of a 'skafto' suggests. This can be seen from the fact that today they fetch high prices, are put back in order and people seem happy enough to live in them. And why not indeed, when the pozzolana from which they are dug is the raw material used for the production of china. What luxury. Besides, the houses are warm in winter and cool in summer, and they are very far from dingy inside. The interior is whitewashed and thus both attracts and reflects the dazzling light of Santorini to such an extent that to sleep on a summer afternoon one has to close all the shutters.

No, the nightmare lay elsewhere: in the living conditions. When eight, 10, 15, or even 20 souls were crammed into those houses, it was the end of any hope of privacy or balance. Most of the little ones, on top of one another, would be screaming and *howling*. And when the family retired for the night, most of the floor space would be occupied... The only fuel for a household of this type was the dried branches of vines and tomato stalks. As we have said, the island is woodless. Cooking involved standing

Today many of the houses are being repaired according to their traditional line and position.

over the fire, feeding it with sticks and getting blackened with soot in the process. Of course, there was no electricity either. There might be a little oil for the lamps, and then the surrounding darkness. Darkness is another of the characteristics of Santorini. As the light is blinding by day, so in the past the darkness was all-enveloping by night. Then not a soul would be abroad in the pitch-black, lonely night. As you walked through the alleyways in the gloom of the pit, in a world with no landscape, you felt yourself alone in the universe. And you would fix your gaze on the pool of light shed by your torch, your only link with the earth, as if watching out for the next step down or up, as if to avoid stumbling.

It is strange, but now, when Santorini is full of people and even has traffic jams at times, there is still one of those alleyways at Fira, with all its isolation and loneliness. They must have forgotten about it. It is the extension of the street which goes from the market to the Gyzis mansion. From that point on and as far as Firostefani, where the road ends, nothing has changed in thirty years. Not even the earthquake touched it. It should be visited in the evening, once darkness has really fallen, and ideally there ought to be a strong wind as well. The whole thing doesn't take more than ten minutes. There may be a street lamp here and there nowadays, but the essence of the place hasn't changed. You will meet no one, and the feeling of awe will be the same as ever it was. Beware, though, not to hurry your step as you pass through; far better just to get accustomed to the idea that you're a being of no importance.

Detail from a neoclassical mansion (Messaria).

Apart from the *skafta*, there were also the houses of the rich, which stood on the flat area at the summit of the hill. They were large, stonebuilt, and plastered, and were sometimes even painted outside with a faint ochre. Their doors and windows were flanked by carved limestone or marble pillars. Above the main entrance of the courtyard there was always a pediment, also in marble, bearing the owner's initials and the date the house was constructed. These edifices were mansions rather than houses. The rich had as many rooms as the poor had children —eighteen, twenty, twenty two— and they had spreading courts around their houses, with cellars underneath for the wine, and stables and byres for the animals, and then the orchards further back, and the fields behind them, stretching as far as the sea itself. The gardener's hut has survived from one of these houses, in a deserted corner of the old garden, as have the painted decorations which adorned the ceiling. Most of these mansions, however, were abandoned after the earthquakes as being unsafe, and have gone to ruin. Fine remains of the houses of the ship-owners can still be seen at Oia. Two or three old houses still stand at Messaria, and at Fira there is one which has been repaired and is lived in. This is the house with the enormous rubber tree opposite the Museum. The islanders who owned these houses had grown rich through trade and shipping. The men of the family travelled to the four corners of the earth, and this can be seen from the interior of any of the old mansions: there will be Viennese furniture, Venetian mirrors, English china and even samovars.

The rich were a small minority, however. In order to understand the occupations of the majority, it must be remembered that, however paradoxical it may seem, the island is a long way from the sea. Fira, the main town, is half an hour from the nearest beach or shore. Until a few years ago there was not one coastal village on the entire island — just a couple of houses at Kamari and perhaps the same number again at Perissa. The villages which stand at Kamari and Perissa today were almost literally built by the tourists. Very few of the islanders were fishermen, and most of them were unable to swim. As for those who in former days came as holiday-makers to Santorini, it is questionable whether they went swimming more than five or six times in the whole summer. There is no deep philosophical explanation behind this. Simply take away the cars from the island as it is today and imagine everyone living in Fira, Merovigli, Apano Meria and Pyrgos. The sea would be inaccessible, and planning, foresight and organization would be needed to go swimming at Kamari. The party would have to be made to agree on a date, the wind would have to be not too strong, and the muleteers would have to be notified and told to bring the right number of animals. Then the whole caravan would set off: two hours to get there, and two hours more to get back. And when you got to Kamari, there would be nothing and no one awaiting you there. Arriving half-broiled by the sun, rugs would be spread on the black sand and hampers would be opened to bring out the meat-balls, the omelettes and the hard-boiled eggs, everything soaked in juice from the tomatoes which had gone soft on the way and sprinkled with crumbs, bits of cheese and sand. How many times each summer would one feel like embarking on such an understaking?

And so the Santorinians lived on the top of their island and most of them were farmers, using their donkeys and mules for work and as a means of transportation. There were very few horses. They have lost their once-predominant role as beasts of burden, and the muleteers —second most important occupation on the island— would certainly have taken up other tourist-oriented professions if it were not for the fact that the animals themselves participate in the tourist fiesta. When the cruise ships land their passengers they do so at the old harbour, at Mesa Yialos, and so the visitors use the traditional means of donkey-power to get themselves up to Fira — cable-car or no cable-car. Anyway, new jobs have been found for the donkeys: some are used to

carry building materials through the cobbled lanes of the villages, while others, with baskets on their backs, do duty as four-legged dustcarts. And so we can see that something, at least, has survived from the past.

These animals are, one might think the only ones on the island. The others, what we might call stock-breeding animals, are nowhere to be seen. Indeed, one would be led to the conclusion that there are none if it were not for the small quantities of goat's-milk cheese (known as *'chloro'* - *'fresh'*) made at Pyrgos and Gonia and the sausage produced in the same villages. Both cheese and sausage are very hard to come by, but worth it when one does. But still it is doubtful if talk of stock-breeding on the island would be justified.

The land is fertile. This pozzolana which turns to a dust the consistency of pepper whenever there is a wind and which blinds you when it blows in your face seems to have almost magical properties. There can be no other explanation for the quality of the island's produce, especially given that apart from anything else it is grown without the benefit of water — who would spare water for the plants on an island as dry as this one? The most important crop is the grape. It is said that the variety grown is the same that once flourished in Monemvasia and from which the legendary Malmsey was made. When the vineyards there fell into ruin, cuttings were taken and planted in Cyprus and Santorini. The truth of the matter is that there are a number of varieties under cultivation, each with its own special name in the local dialect, and all of them are of the very finest quality — as is the wine made

from them. In the past the only types of wine known were the red, dry *'brusco'*, the *'Bordeaux'*-type wines, the 'night-wine' (see below) and the sweet red wine from sun-dried grapes called visanto — from vino sancto, or Communion wine.

All the wine was home-produced. You went with your demijohn to Evangelou's cellar or to the *Dominicans* — huge vaulted cellars beneath the biggest mansions, like underground railway stations. To the right and left would be the barrels and at the far end the wine-press. In front of this would stand the two tanks in which the must was gathered. The cellars really came to life just after the feast of the Dormition of the Virgin, on August 15. This was the time the grapes were harvested, and during which the island was a hive of activity. The donkeys would spend all day on the road from the vineyard to the cellars, each carrying two large baskets for the fruit. The work in the vineyard was done by both men and women, from sunrise to sunset, while in the cellars there would be more men —women did not usually take part in this task— with their trouser-legs rolled up a little higher than usual, their hands clasped behind their backs and their bodies leaning forward as they rhythmically trampled the grapes. One can imagine what fun the trampling of the grapes was for the children — there was nothing to compare with the ticklish feeling on the soles of the feet as one trod, not to mention the literally intoxicating atmosphere produced by the fumes. The only slightly unpleasant sensation was to stand in a footmark just mady by someone else and still warm. One of the Santorini wines was made from untrodden grapes: the last loads brought each evening by the muleteers and which would be trampled next morning lay all night heaped in the press, which caused the grapes to burst of their own accord and the juice to run out. This juice was collected in a special container and from it the 'night wine' ('nychteri') was made.

Most of the cellars survived the earthquake and are easy to visit as they have become restaurants and discos. And there are still some people who cultivate the vine. Perhaps someone will have the thought while there is time of taking a few cuttings and planting them somewhere else, as happened with the Malmsey vineyards all those centuries ago.

If one excepts the grape -and barley, which is grown as animal food, there is something peculiar about all the agricultural produce of Santorini. Take the tomatoes, for instance — the second most important crop on the island. But what kind of tomatoes, that's the question. Today you find cherries which are bigger than Santorini tomatoes. The size of the marbles we played with as children, their skin is tough and their taste unbelievable — as if someone had manage to condense into this tiny mass all the taste of a large tomato. The tomato puree, of course, which was made from these tomatoes was of equivalent magnificence. Before the earthquake there were nine factories on the island making puree and canning it. They may have been seasonal factories, only working during the harvest, but there were nine of them. In how many other parts of Greece was such harmony between agricultural and industrial production to be found? Now they have fallen into disuse. The earthquake, one might think, until one sees that their chimneys are still in position. The earthquake is not to blame —what is at fault is the fall in tomato production. There is only one factory left, belonging to the Co-operative, and during the harvest season it works one day in three. To put it another way, tomato production has fallen by a factor of 27, or by 96%.

The tomatoes are so small as to be difficult to pick, but it's worth the effort.

Cleaning the fava.

Another of the strange products is the chick-pea (fava in Greek). What is strange about it is that it is relatively rare and that one never sees it in its virgin state — before it goes into the grinder, that is to say. Even when you do manage to catch a glimpse of it, it is difficult to describe. It's a pulse, smaller than a dried pea, about the same colour as lentils and completely irregular in shape — rather like a large grain of sand. Indeed if you were to take a few chick-peas and mix them up with some equally dark sand from Kamari, you wouldn't be able to tell one from the other. This might not be a good moment for such an experiment, mind you, what with the scarcity of chick-peas in recent years — they really shouldn't be wasted. Even more pecular are the fruit and vegetables —such as they are, from the point of view of quantity— grown on the island. The aubergines are white. There are white water-melons, too —the meat of the fruit, not its skin— with jet-black pips.

From what we have seen so far, it will be plain that one shouldn't expect to find in Santorini the things which are normally considered traditional articles — wood-carvings, cloth, pottery or ironwear. We are, of course, talking of things native to the island. There is a little basket-weaving with wicker — the baskets the animals carry, for instance, and those things like muzzles that they put over the snouts of the mules. One may come across the odd hand grinder for chick-peas, or wooden utensils for the wine-cellar, or perhaps a stone mortar and pestle. That is all. Apart from foodstuffs, Santorini has no traditional products. Tradition is to be found elsewhere, not in the shops, and of necessity you will leave it where you found it. It is not of the sort that can be taken away.

First of all, the tradition of Santorini will be found in its cooking. The most accessible of the traditional features of the island it its false meat-balls — 'pseftokeftedes'. These are made of nothing at all — and certainly not of meat, necessity being the mother of invention. The raw material is a kind of batter made of flour, tomato juice, plenty of grated onion, plenty of mint and whatever other vegetable matter happens to be in the house and would otherwise be thrown away, all ground up. Fry the batter as you would a fritter and it becomes one of the nicest things you've ever tasted. But bear in mind that Santorini keeps jealous guard even over something as insignificant as false meat-balls. If you try making it anywhere else, with tomatoes which aren't from Santorini, you'll be wasting your time.

Unknown local builders with an innate artistic sense were the creators of these marvellous pieces of architecture.

Anyone wanting more features of tradition has only to look around him. We have already described the way the houses were built. What is characteristic of the villages as a whole is that there is not one straight line in them. Not even the vaults are symmetrical. Just take a look at the walls on the precipice side of the streets, and you will see that not even the ones built recently with concrete-blocks and cement are the same width all along their length. This plethora of asymmetrical straight lines, meeting to form the most unlikely shapes, is what gives to the masses of the buildings a sweetness and gentleness which are surprising

on such an island. It would seem that without really intending to the islanders gave their home precisely what nature had deprived it of — tenderness.

Oia

The churches are out of all proportion to the humble villages in which they stand. They occupy a great deal of space, are imposing, and irrespective of whether they are Orthodox or Catholic always combine both local and western features, as is also the case in Syros. Some are glaring white, some are painted ochre; some are basilicas and others are in the form of a Byzantine cross; they almost always have domes and two bell-towers in the facade like old-style cathedrals. The domes are painted white or azure emulsion or even a light turquoise which has nothing Greek about it. By way of complete contrast, the western monasteries are western in style: massive, strongly-built, with quadrangles and arches and always painted ochre — fortresses of the faith.

Over and above the architecture and, of course, the religion itself, the Catholic element also had and continues to have various cultural influences on the island. These features, which might perhaps best be called western rather than Catholic, are to be encountered where one least expects them and are always a surprise. Who would have thought, for instance, that the islanders of Santorini would make Christmas puddings just like they do in Britain? The name has been corrupted, of course, to the French-sounding 'bouden', but the recipe and the taste are just the same. They also make 'nioki', which is Italian. And then there are the names: Sarlos (Charles), Virzini (Virginia), Flora, Guillaime or Guglielmos, Clotidi (or Klotida in dialect) — the last two were a couple, at that. And what about Oreli, from Aurelie? There were even French nick-names: there was the boatman known, perhaps maliciously, as Loudeme, from loup de mer, which means sea-wolf. Nor was it unknown for Russian names to rub shoulders with the French ones: Annushka, Kolia. Presumably these arrived along with the samovars. And, of course, there were the local names, that is to say, the Greek names which the locals had a preference for: Minas and Markos for the men and Maroulidi, or Maroulio for the women. The latter of these comes fromthe charming name Amaryllis.

The language and accent of Santorini constitute another element in its tradition. Along general lines, the dialect is reminiscent of Cretan, but the careful listener will, as in other parts of Greece, come across a multitude of ancient elements which have survived and which co-exist with others which arrived directly from the west. Apart from these, which are easy for the Greek-speaker to collect and study, there are the images and expressions peculiar to every part of Greece which appear for a moment in the course of speech and then are lost, perhaps for ever. Once a boatman preparing to set out on a long voyage was asked what he thought of the weather:

— "It looks thoughtful, squire", was his reply.

Or again, the island lady who asked:

— "Stuffed, then squire?"

When she wanted to know if her master had taken breakfast.

The songs of the Santorinians, although they too are beginning to be forgotten, are less transient. The songs were sung at feasts and celebrations which, if the truth be told, were held ususally in the morning and concentrated more on food than on dancing and singing. Each saint had a dish of his own, from which he took his name. St. George 'Sfoungatas', for instance, was celebrated by the making of *'sfoungato'* - omelettes. As throughout the Cyclades, the Santorini dance is that known as the 'ballos'. The chief instruments are the laouto —a form of lute, as its name suggests— and the violin. What was unique was the island song, a couplet set to a local melody and full of the ancient and unrequited passion for love and money. These songs are given here in prose translation;

Rich men, make money
to take with you
For Charon buys no souls
on credit.

Rain-drop by rain-drop holes
are worn in the marble,
A love which won't be taken
isn't worth loving.

When four eyes and two hearts
are in love
Better for death to take them
than to separate.

Lastly, there are the songs which, again in couplets, the islanders may sing at any moment in their lives, whether they are muleteers walking up from Yialos through the blazing heat or revellers returning home through the summer dark, and which are heard despite the pangs of hunger or the threat of earthquake. There is, for instance, a couplet which all the Greeks since the time of the Persian Wars and perhaps earlier must have sung to themselves:

Patience, patience,
wait and watch
Every road which climbs
one day goes down.

Only belief of this kind can explain why this place is still on its feet.

ROUTES ON SANTORINI

1. Fira: Southern and Northern part
2. Fira - Volcano - Thirasia
3. Fira - Oia (Apano Meria)
4. Fira - Pyrgos - Profitis Ilias Monastery
5. Fira - Monolithos
6. Fira - Kamari - Mesa Vouno
7. Fira - Karterados - Athinios - Perissa
8. Fira - Akrotiri

ROUTE 1

Fira

Fira is the capital of Santorini, with a population of about 1,650, with a Cathedral, a high school, banks, a large luxury hotel, a doctor's surgery, a wide range of shops and even an art gallery. The capital is among Santorini's most recent communities, with barely two centuries of life behind it. It came into being in the late 18th century, when circumstances no longer obliged the islanders to live high up on the inaccessible parts of the islands. At that time *Skaros* was still the most important fortified centre (see route 3). But its inhabitants began to look around for somewhere else to live, in a flatter spot with some sort of access to the sea. Skaros was gradually abandoned and the new capital grew.

There has been much controversy over the origin of the name 'Fira'. It is normally argued that it is derived from Thera, the ancient name of the island. But this view runs into opposition from some linguists, who derive Fira from the adjective 'pyrros' which means reddish, flame-coloured, or even yellowish, and which has come into modern Greek as 'fyrros' or 'fyros', with the same meaning and is widely used in island placenames. According to this theory, which is in the end more convincing, the town's

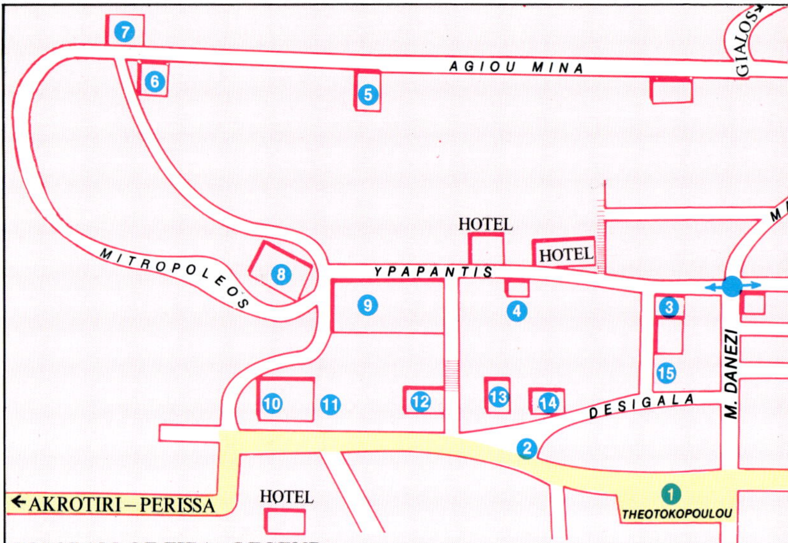

DIAGRAM OF FIRA - LEGEND
1 Theotokopoulou Square: bus terminal and starting-point for our routes. 2 Taxis. 3 Theoxenia Hotel. 4 Telephone company (OTE). 5 Church of St. John. 6 Customs house. 7 Church of St. Minas. 8 Atlantis Hotel. 9 Orthodox Cathedral. 10 Olympic

name really ought to be spelt 'Fyra'. We have chosen to stick to the other form, which has been established for very many years now. For the same reason, we have spelt the island 'Santorini' instead of the more correct form 'Santorene' - after all, the name does include the word 'eirene' (Irene).

Fira is a long and narrow community, with its main axis running north-south. It stands on the lip of the caldera and is encircled by two streets. The more westerly of these (Agiou Mina St. and its extension M. Nomikou St.) lies as it were over the precipice, while that to the east, Erythrou Stavrou St., runs inland and has no view whatever. Between these two streets along the edge of the town is a third, the main street and axis of the town. This is Ipapantis St., which is extended to the south by Mitropoleos St., while to the north it is interrupted by the beginning of M. Nomikou St., which runs at right angles to it. But still further north there is another street, Ayiou Ioannou St., which could be described as the continuation of the main street (see the plan of the town of Fira above. As these streets run north they converge, finally coming together in Firostefani Square.

There are no cars in Fira. All the streets which we have mentioned are narrow and cobbled, with steps and sudden rises. In bygone days they were covered with a thick layer of dried dung, which may have been unhygienic but made walking as soft as if you were treading on a rug. Now the streets are clean; the years have

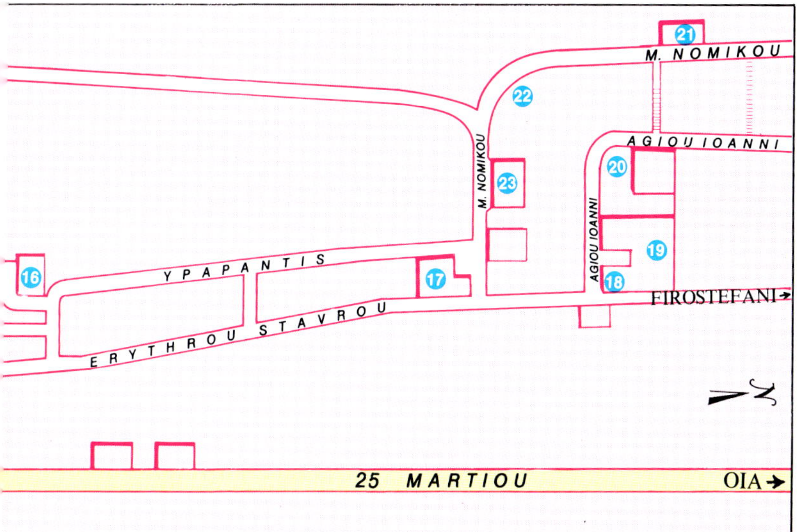

Airways. 11 Folklore and Historical Museum. 12 Post Office. 13 Chemist's shop. 14 Banks. 15 Harbourmaster's Office. 16 'The Club': newsagents. 17 Archaeological Museum. 18 Gyzis Mansion (Arts Centre). 19 Catholic monasteries. 20 Catholic church. 21 Church of St. Stylianos. 22 'Patsouli'. 23 Cable-car.

swept away the dung.

A fourth street, parallel to the other three and properly surfaced, runs to the east of the town. This is 25 March St., which really forms part of the main road axis crossing the island from north to south (from Oia to Perissa). Approximately halfway along Fira this road widens out and forms a narrow square, also running north-south: Theotokopoulou Square, where the buses and taxis start from, and forever bustling with people and motion. We shall take this square as the starting-point for our itineraries on the island (see routes 3-8) and for the measurement of distances (in kilometres). In the case of the tour of Fira and for the trip to the caldera and the Volcano (route 2), however, we shall start from elsewhere: from the intersecton of Michail Danezi and Ipapantis Sts.

Michail Danezi St., which lies at right angles to the four parallel streets we have already mentioned, starts in the NW corner of the square. We follow it untill the point at which it cuts across Ipapantis St: this intersection is the starting-point for our itinerary. Danezi St., is behind us, and in front are the first steps of Marinatou St., which leads down, with steps all the way, to Mesa Yialos, the island's former port (see route 2), better known as *'dromos tou Yialou'* (the road to the sea). To our right and left, Ipapantis St; the left leg leads to the southern part of Fira, and the right to the northern part. In a similar manner, our itinerary will be split into two parts.

Ipapantis St.

Ayios Minas

A. Fira - Southern Part

This is a walk best taken in the morning, before the sun has risen too high.

We walk along Ipapantis St. There are shops on both sides of the street, and the Theoxenia hotel on the left. After the hotel there is a street on the left leading to the square. The street we are on has begun to widen. On the right, the buildings begin to thin out and there are considerable sections of street with an uninterrupted view over the precipice. We pass the telephone company offices (OTE), on our left, and reach the art gallery 'I Palaia Fambrika' (The old Factory). Depending on one's mood, one can either go into the gallery or sit on the low wall (locally, *'boundi'*) to admire the landscape.

The landscape is one of the main attractions of this route, and it is perhaps the most characteristic of the whole island: this is the view shown on most postcards, book-covers, posters and advertisements. The church of Ayios (St.) Minas, on the tip of the rock to our left has become something of a symbol of Santorini. Directly in front of us is a complex of blindingly white courtyards, flat roofs, and steps, in the foreground and middle ground, leading interminably on down into the distance as they follow the slope of the precipice, each house standing lower than the one closer to us than it. The last line of houses has for a background the sea which lies two hundred and fifty metres further down. What made the original builders of that last line of houses choose sites right above the

FRANCO

In the foreground, the fine church of St. John in Kato Fira.

maelstrom? Presumably we shall never know.

To our left, the view is enclosed by Akrotiri, which extends like a snake to embrace the caldera. To our right, in the background, Thirasia. And in the centre of the caldera is the Volcano, like a huge blackish sleeping sea beast. It once snowed in Santorini and everyone wondered whether the snow would lie on the volcano, too; fortunately the snow stopped soon, for the sight would have been ludicrous — a white volcano, like a photographic negative.

A few metres beyond the wall on which we are sitting is the start of a path winding downhill with broad steps, which will bring us closer to the houses and courtyards we have been looking at from above. This part of town is known, from its position, as **Kato** (Lower) **Fira**. As we go down we approach a church of St. John, on our right. Our elevated position enables us to get a bird's eye view of its floor plan, admiring as we do the variety and conjunction of the masses which go to make it up. The dome is supported on an eight-sided drum, with one window in each side; it is very rarely that one can see, as one does here thanks to the position of the church relative to the road, a building of this kind from top to bottom, and that is surely the reason for which the local builders took particular care over the exterior decoration of the church. The eight sides of the drum are of dark-coloured and striking limestone, which sets them off, and at the base of the cross there is a decorative motif carved in the shape of a star which would be entirely pointless if the passer-by were not so close to the top of the dome.

After a turn of 180°, the street leads into the courtyard of the church and from there to Ayiou Mina St., on the edge of the precipice. We continue to the left, losing ourselves in the backstreets of Kato Fira — a different world, quiet and remote, with a pace of its own, only a few yards from the bustle and noise of the upper town. We reach the church of Ayios Minas, with its typically Santorinian dome, composed of three elements: a) the polyhedral drum with one opening in each side; b) the dome itself, with one or two rows of obtruding stones (string-courses) which make it reminscent of a mine, and c) the turret on top of the keystone of the dome, also consisting of a polyhedral drum with openings and a second, smaller, dome bearing the cross.

From here on our street turns left and begins to run uphill once more to bring us back to the level of Ipapantis St., which we reach after passing the third church on our route, that of the Transformation of the Saviour, with its fine iron gratings on the windows. We arrive at the top and enter Mitropoleos St., which is the continuation of Ipapantis St. We turn left (that is to say, in a northerly direction) to return to the point from which we started. Number 12 in this street is the mansion of the Metropolitan. We continue, past the large hotel Atlantis on our left, after which the road widens (as the beginning of Ipapantis St.) and to our right rises the Orthodox Cathedral of Santorini, dedicated to Ipapanti, (the Coming of Christ into the Temple), with the same feastday as that of the Purification of the Virgin in the Roman Church. The Cathedral is also known as Our Lady 'Belonia'.

The Cathedral dominates the town.

Belonias was the name of the builder of the first church on this site in 1827, and initially it belonged to his family. In the early part of this century it was renovated and donated to the Municipality of Santorini. It was an imposing structure, painted ochre and with two tall bell-towers in its facade, to the right and left of the main entrance. It dominated the landscape. In the earthquakes, the building was totally destroyed and another, quite different, erected on its site. While the first church imposed itself by means of its height, the present building does so with its mass and its width, a contribution also being made by the large courtyard and the colonnade. On the outside it is white, the windows and the colonnade being the only decoration. The interior, however, has very interesting murals, the work of Christophoros Asimis, who also painted all the murals in the church of St. Haralambos at Exo Gonia (see route 4). Work has not yet finished on Our Lady 'Belonia'.

Directly after the church, the road leads right to the Post Office and the banks.

Our walk is over, and we return to our starting point.

The Cathedral bell-tower.

B. Fira - Northern Part

Starting from the same crossroads at which the previous walk began, we climb the broad steps of which Ipapantis St., to the right, consists. Shops, mostly selling souvenirs, line the street on both sides. Ipapantis St., always had shops; it might be called the best commercial area in Fira, not the market itself: this is where the drapers' and shoe shops were, the Notary Public's office, the news-agents, and other similar establishments. At the top, standing at right angles to the street, is the *"Club"*, with its marble entrance and carved pediment. The building was inititally used as a gambling club, and this is where it got its name. Later it became a kind of coffee-shop, with billiard tables, and today it has a double purpose: the main entrance and the right-hand portion serve as newsagent's, and the larger left-hand part, has been converted into a bookshop (the view over the caldera from the balcony is very fine). The inscription on the pediment of the Club informs us that the building dates from 1871. The name of the builder cannot be seen: the marble plaque giving the name of the owner of the newsagent's has covered it up.

We continue along our way, bypassing the Club and climbing north (at the point where we detour round the Club there is a stairway to the right leading into a parallel street where the market is. It is worth spending some time in the alleyways near here, with their shops, restaurants and bars).

Marinatou St.

An alleyway in the area of the market.

HOTEL
LUCAS
Taverna
Fantasia

To our left, the fact that the houses stand at a level quite a bit lower than the road allows us to enjoy the view out to sea. As we ascend we shall see three interesting examples of the old mansion-house style of the island. The first, at no, 66, is that of the Sarpakis family, and is in a semi-ruinous state. The two wings of the house occupied the space both to the right and the left of the road. The left wing, of which we see the roof, extended under the street and communicated with the right wing, which stands higher. At no. 76 is the Nomikos house, with the same arrangement vis-a-vis the road as the other house we have been describing. It is, however, more modern, having been built after the earthquake on the site of an older building. The third house is that of the Vazengiou family, which stands in M. Nomikou street, which intersects with Ipapandis St., and ends there. The main entrance to the house, adorned by an enormous rubber tree, is exactly opposite Ipapandis St. The Vaxengiou house was repaired after the earthquake and has reverted to its original form. Perhaps it is the last of the old Santorini mansions still to be lived in.

On the right-hand of Ipapandis and M. Nomikou Sts., is the Archaeological Museum, on the site of the old National Bank, of which only the aged palm in the garden has survived.

Fira from Merovigli.

The Archaeological Museum

The **Archaeological Museum of Fira** has on display mainly finds from the excavations at Mesa Vouno conducted by Friedrich Hiller von Goertringen between 1896 and 1900. There have also finds and private collections dating from the period previous to this dig and finds from the more recent investigation of the Akrotiri site by archaeologist Spyros Marinatos. (See route 6 for Mesa Vouno and route 8 for Akrotiri). Among the more important exhibits are the following:

— marble figurines dating from the 3rd millenium BC
— statuettes of women, of a devotional nature
— marble 'kouroi' (statues of young men)
— bas reliefs and statues from Hellenistic and Roman times
— Archaic vessels from Mesa Vouno, mostly of the 'kylix' (cup) type, with painted representations of triremes and horses
— scythus-type cups from Akrotiri
— pithos jars from Mesa Vouno and Akrotiri.

Many of the finds from Akrotiri have been moved to Athens, and are to be seen in the Archaeological Museum there.

An ancient vessel decorated in relief (Fira Archaeological Museum).

The statue of Aphrodite in Fira Archaeological Museum.

Balcony of a restored mansion.

After visiting the Museum, we take the short downhill stretch of M. Nomikou St., (eastwards), reaching Erythrou Stavrou St., and turning left (north). This street, as we see it from the spot at which we stand, with its barrel vaulting and the crossbeams which roof it at various points, is among the most picturesque spots on the island and is a favourite subject for painters and photographers. At no. 182, on the right, is the marble entry of another old mansion, that of the Koutsoyannopoulos family. Over the entrance are the initials of the first owner, G.K.M., and the date of construction, 1882. Directly opposite Ayiou Ioannou St. climbs up at right angles to Erythrou Stavrou St. The Gyzis mansion stands on the right-hand corner of Ayiou Ioannou and Erythrou Stavrou Sts.

Detail of an interior wall.

The entrance to the Gyzis mansion.

The courtyard of the Gyzis mansion.

The **Gyzis Mansion** (17th century) is one of the oldest buildings in Fira. Today it belongs to the Catholic bishopric, which has restored it and given it new uses to make it once more part of the life of the town. It is used as an arts centre, with a hall suitable for events of all kinds and exhibition rooms.

We enter a white-painted courtyard surrounded by the high wings of the building. The light is so strong on Santorini, and its reflection from the white walls so blinding, that it is nearly impossible to believe one is in the shade. Note the arches which surround the yard and form part of its decoration, hewn from dark-coloured limestone in sharp contrast to the white-washed walls. On the western side of the courtyard, a door leads to what was the vintage of the house, which has been converted into a theatre-like hall without spoiling either the grape press (on the left as we enter) or the tanks into which the grape juice ran. The main entrance to the house, which today leads to the exhibition rooms, is on the north side of the courtyard.

The Gyzis Mansion comes alive in the summer thanks to the various events (theatrical performances, concerts and exhibitions) which take place there. Details of these events can be obtained on the spot only.

We leave the Gyzis Mansion and also Erythrou Stavrou St., which continues northward, deserted and lonely now, in the direction of Firostefani. For those who are fond of solitude, the walk from here to the square in Firostefani is a fine one. We shall take Ayiou Ioannou St. This is the main street of the Catholic quarter.

The convent carpet-weaving shop.

The Domos belfry.

Immediately after the Gyzis Mansion, there is a raised area which gives access to two Catholic convents. On the left, once we are on this raised area, is the imposing entry to the Convent of the Sisters of Mercy, who settled on Santorini in 1841. The convent once had a school, a hospital and a dispensary run by the nuns. All this came to an end with the earthquakes, at which time the nuns left the island. Most of the convent has been restored, and houses the offices of the Catholic see, a hostel for groups of young people from abroad and a very interesting carpet-weaving workshop where girls from the island learn the painstaking task of rug-making. The convent and the factory can be visiting during working hours.

At the far side of the raised area is the entry to the convent of the Dominican nuns. Dominican nuns, it will be remembered, live in complete retreat and for this reason the convent is not open to visitors. To its right, however, is its church, the 'Rozaria', which is open to visitors and is well worth it, too, as a fine example of the combination of the island's style and the Baroque.

Returning to Ayiou Ioannou St., the bell-tower of the *"Domos"*, the church of St. John the Baptist, the Catholic cathedral, rises on our right. The church was severely damaged in the earthquake, and although it has been restored much of the Baroque element in its interior decoration has not been renewed. We continue, with the convent of the Sisters of Mercy on our right. The road runs under enormous arches at some points, and soon turns right, in a northerly direction. Now it is more or less an extension of Ipapandis St., which had been

The chapel of St. Stylianos.

interrupted by the Vaxengiou mansion and the Domos which stands directly behind it. We can go only a little further before coming to a narrow roadway with steps leading to the edge of the precipice.

To our right at this point is the entrance to the island's third Catholic monastery, that of the Lazarists, and also the entrance to the monastery church. The monastery is undergoing restoration and is at present closed.

We walk down the narrow street with the steps and come out on to the road running along the edge of the precipice. We are back in M. Nomikou St. Before turning left to complete our peregrination and find ourselves back where we started, it is worth taking a couple of steps to the right to see, the church of St. Stylianos, a lilliputeian structure clinging grimly to the edge of the road so as not to slide off into the precipice. The road continues north to the "Frangika" quarter and from there to Firostefani.

We return, and walk along M. Nomikou St., to the point at which it turns left. This spot is known as "**Patsouli**" and the view from it is absolutely astounding. For many people, it is the most beautiful place on the island. It is certainly the most romantic, with its incomparable view down over the road to Yialos, Limanaki, and Trypes (see route 2). For those who remember it, this spot is redolent of the festivities of the past: groups of merry-makers would assemble at dawn down at Yialos and make their way up on foot, while others would be waiting for them at the top, at Patsouli, both groups singing —those at the top somewhat sarcastically, those on the way up with stolidity— the same song:

Patience, patience,
wait and watch
every road which climbs
one day goes down

One can spend hours at Patsouli just waiting for the sun to set. In any case, our walk is over. A little further along to the left is the entrance to the cable-car, and the Vaxengiou mansion is directly after that. We are back where we began.

Fira from Patsouli

ZORBAS

ROUTE 2

Fira - Mesa Yialos - Volcano - Thirasia - Oia (Apano Meria)

Part of this itinerary will involve the use of the boat which does the trip round the caldera. Before starting, find out the times of the trips and, if you wish, pre-purchase tickets from one of the agencies in Fira. There are normally two trips a day, one in the morning and one in mid-afternoon, the morning run lasting longer. Stout shoes and socks are essential to permit comfortable walking on the volcano. It is also a good idea to have a snack and a bottle of water with one, especially if taking the morning trip.

Donkeys and their passengers ascend the 'dromos tou Yialou'.

We start (an hour before the time the boat leaves will be more than enough) from the same crossroads we used for the visit to Fira (see route 1) and we shall take Spyrou Marinatou St., directly in front of us. The first part of the itinerary is the descent of the precipice down to sea level, on foot. The pathway spirals down, consisting of 587 broad steps (about two paces for each them). Each straight section between bends is known as a *"vena"* (pural "venes"), some of which have names: Alonakia (the little threshing floors), Gria Spilia (the old cave), Papoutsa. At one time this roadway was the sole connection between the island and the ships, and mules were the sole means of transport for goods and people. Today, with the motor road to Athinios, the *Yialos road* has remained one of the most attractive places on Santorini: first, because of its setting, second, because of the donkey ride necessary to re-ascend, and third because the bay at which the road ends is a very beautiful one. Cruise boats continue to land their passengers at Mesa Yialos, and the cableway has its terminus there.

At the start of our itinerary we walk through the lower houses of Fira, most of which have been converted into souvenir shops, coffee-shops and restaurants.

Early-morning visitors to Mesa Yialos will encounter the fishermen.

But the houses become sparser and sparser, and we gradually realise that the walls of the crater are all around us. Now we are seeing the caldera not from above, but from the inside, and we can stop and observe the various geological strata of which it consists: brown, reddish, and grey, and as we descend the volcano become larger and larger until it completely fills the horizon.

It takes about twenty minutes to walk to the bottom. **Mesa Yialos** is a picturesque little harbour with its houses, its coffee-shops and its jetty. It would be just like every other little port in the Cyclades if it were not for the towering precipice above it and if that precipice did not continue into the sea. Indeed, a glance from the edge of the quay will show just how deep the water is and how quickly it takes on a dark blue colour. How could a boat possibly anchor there? Just a little out from the beach the water is sixty metres deep. Boats can be moored only to the buoys to be seen here and there in the bay.

On the northern side of the bay the yellowish cliff plunging down from on high has been eroded by the sea and there are caves at its base. They look rather like broken-down skafta houses which have sunk into the water. They gave the place its name — Trypes (the holes). The building with the battlements which dominates this corner is of recent construction. The starting-point for the cable-car is near Trypes.

Only when you're down at the bottom can you really feel what it means to be there...

We have a little time to walk around the south side of the bay. The first place we come to is Limanaki, formed by a little jetty running parallel to the shore behind which are moored the boats that once brought passengers ashore from the Piraeus ships and which now, motorized, do the same job for the cruise liners. A little further along is the pretty chapel of St. Nicholas. As we walk along we see on our left the ruins of an old tomato processing factory, immediately after which there is a narrow path to a little jetty at the southernmost end of the bay. This is the **Lazaretta**, where in days past those suspect of harbouring disease were quarantined. Swimming is possible here; the water is relatively safe for some way out. Care should be taken not to get too far from the shore and not to swim when there is a strong wind. We return to the central quay of Yialos and board the boat.

Our boat starts off in a westerly direction and heads for the north harbour of the volcano. As we look around, we get a general idea of the walls of the caldera, with the white fringe of Fira on top. Balades, the place where the pozzolana is mined and its installations for loading ships begin to appear on the right. From here it is easy to see the extent of the damage that the exploitation of its ground has done to the island.

After about five or six minutes, the depth of the sea beneath us is more or less the same as the height that Fira stands above Yialos: 300 metres, give or take a little. After this the water becomes much shallower, especially to the left of the boat as we go forward. At this point there is an outcrop of the sea bottom which permits the larger ships to fall back upon it and this is where the cruise ships stop. The spot is known as 'pangos'.

Now we are close to the **volcano**, and the first mass of black lava can be seen to the right. It can easily be seen from the appearance of the lava that the black material issued forth from the ground in viscous form, cooling suddenly and retaining the form it had on its emission. It gives one a fair idea of what hell must be like... This lava, 'tis Dafnis' as it is called, is relatively recent, and dates only from the 1925-26 eruption. As we enter the little harbour in which we shall disembark, the water begins to take on a green opaque look produced by the sulphur. Later we shall have the opportunity to swim around our moored boat, and it will be seen that the water is lukewarm.

For the moment, we leave the boat and take the uphill path to the crater. The whole trip, there and back, takes about an hour. The first thing we shall see is a fig tree, believe it or not, standing as if representing some vain endeavour of Nature to give the landscape a peaceful note. Afer the fig tree there is nothing but lava.

The crater is perhaps the least awe-inspiring feature of the volcano. It resembles a gigantic basin of pozzolana, on whose lip we stand. Not, of course, that the crater does not provoke a certain measure of awe, the proof of this being the silence which comes across the group of visitors when they first see it and also the fact that no one dares to go down to the bottom. Around us sulphurous smoke is emitted at a number of points. Elsewhere the ground and the stones are hot to the touch. If one is lucky, it is possible that on lifting a stone the bright yellow crystals of sulphur will be seen adhering to its bottom. We return to the shore and have time for a swim, which is a blessing after the dust, earth and heat of the volcano.

Leaving behind the volcano, our boat now heads for Thirasia, the independent part of the caldera which forms its north-western wall. During the voyage we shall be able to observe the two separate islands which make up the volcano: Nea Kameni which

Fira from the volcano.

The crater of the volcano.

The interior of the caldera is a place of wild, proud and imposing beauty.

we have just been visiting, and behind it, long and narrow, Palaia Kameni, which had been fully formed by 1508 (see the table of eruptions on p. 19).

Thirasia is the second largest island of the complex which forms the caldera. It is 5.7 km long and 2.7 km wide at its widest point. There are, however, only 245 inhabitants. Isolated from the main mass of the island, Thirasia has not followed the rapid course of its development. The population consists mostly of farmers who till the fertile western plain and produce grapes, tomatoes, chick-peas and barley. The main village bears the same name as the island, and is built on the rim of the precipice, which is not so high at this point: 145 steps are sufficient to bring one to the top. The village itself reminds one ot the other villages on Santorini: the same cobbled streets, the same architecture, the same view. There is another village inland, Potamos, with a population of 93. Lastly there is Agrilia; population: 0.

On the south side of the island there is a double-ended cave, known as Tripiti, near the sea. The north end of the island must hide interesting antiquities which have not been investigated so far. This is where the little chapel of St. Irene (Ayia Eirini) stands, which, according to many, gave Santorini its name, contesting with the St. Irene of Perissa for this honour (see route 7).

The boat trip does not usually include time for a walk up to Thirasia and a visit to all the island. What is most usual is for there to be a stop at

Thirasia: the harbour from above.

the bay for a swim and a snack on the beach or near the white chapel of Zoodochos Piyi.

Next our boat will cross the strait which separates Thirasia from **Apano Meria** (just over a mile) and will stop at one of the latter's two beaches, **Ammoudi** or **Armeni**. Apano Meria is one of the most interesting parts of Santorini, and we shall be coming back via the land to pay it a more detailed visit (see route 3). All we shall get today is a general picture of the landscape from the sea.

When we leave Apano Meria we are on the return leg of our trip. We sail along the caldera from N to S, and can see all the wild beauty of the strata of which Santorini is made up, with the rock of Skaros, like an enormous stone castle rising out of the sea, in the middle. The little white dot to be discerned high up on Skaros is the 'Theoskepasti' chapel (see route 3).

When we arrive back at Mesa Yialos we have two possibilities as far as going back up to Fira is concerned: the donkeys and the cable-car. Perhaps we may choose the donkeys this time, as being more colourful, and use the cable-car on another occasion for a second —and impressive— trip to Mesa Yialos and a quick swim at Lazaretta.

Apano Meria.

ROUTE 3

Fira - Oia (Apano Meria) Returning along the NE Coast

Fira - Oia: 11.7 km Total route: 24.5 km.

Via: Fira - Firostefani - Nunnery of St. Nicholas - Imerovigli - Finikia - Perivolos - Oia.

Return via: Tholos - Baxedes - Koloumbos - Our Lady 'tou Kalou' - Vourvoulos - Kontochori - Fira.

The road from Fira to Oia is surfaced. That for the return is not, but the track usually presents few difficulties.

A different view at every corner (Firostefani).

The main interest of this route is that it includes all the villages built on the lip of the precipice and looking down into the caldera: Firostefani, Imerovigli and Oia. The route will acquaint the visitor with the volcanic nature of the island —which is its most notable feature— and will provide him with a unique view from a number of different angles. The trip can be combined with a swim, either at one, ofthe beaches of Oia or at one of the countless beaches along the NE coast, which are almost deserted, as well.

0.0 km. From the square in Fira we take the road which runs towards the northern part of the island. The town of Fira lies to our left, merging into the village of Firostefani, whose square we reach after 800 metres.

0.8 km. Firostefani. Some people claim that the name of the village is a corruption of Firon Stefani. If what we have said about Fira is true (see p. 47) and if we take into account that 'stefani' can also mean 'rock' (its normal meaning is 'wreath' or 'hoop') then the name of the village means 'red rock'. However the case may be, Firostefani is an extension of Fira and, on a different scale of course, could be thought of as the northern suburbs of the capital. The village is long and narrow, standing on the edge of the precipice, and has its own square, restaurant, hotels, coffee-shop, and a large and impressive church, of St. Gerasimos, which —unusually for the island— is flanked by tall cypresses.

Firostefani has a marvellous view of the caldera, different to that from Fira. The cliff here is much steeper, and the particularly picturesque features of the path with its steps and the little harbour at Mesa Yialos do not come between the visitor and the view as they do at Fira. To the right is the island's most elegant and resplendant rock mass, Skaros. The volcano has changed shape: behind it and to the right the long, narrow mass of Palia Kameni, parallel to the sea, can be distinguished. As we walk N from the square, we enter the main part of the village. To the left, the

If the little taverna is shut, it'll have opened by the time you've looked at the view.

Merovigli, on the lip of the crater.

ruins of two old windmills. Further along and also to the left, two lanes lead to the sloping part of the village, built on the side of the cliff. This section of the village has now been completely restored and there is an especially fine variety of shapes, masses and colours created by the courtyards, roofs and protruding portions of the 'skafta' houses as we see them from above. We return to the square.

The road leading S from the square along the lip of the precipice goes to Fira. After some 50 metres, the Catholic church of Firostefani (Our Lady of the Saints Theodore) which has its feast day on August 15. From the church to Fira the inhabitants are mostly Catholic. This is the area known as 'Frangika' (see also p. 62). The view is superb.

Firostefani can of course be reached on foot from Fira. Start from Patsouli taking the road along the precipice through Frangika, or take the road described on p. 62.

We return to our transport. The road continues N through the fields.

1.4. km. Nunnery of St. Nicholas. The St. Nicholas nunnery was founded in 1651 by the Gyzis family, one of the few Orthodox families living at that time in the Skaros castle (see below, Imerovigli, Skaros). It was originally located on Skaros, and it operated there without interruption until 1815. When the castle settlement fell into disuse, the nuns decided to move, founding a new establishment in a more accessible spot, and this was the site they chose.

The new nunnery was built between 1819 and 1821, with the expenditure of considerable effort and 90,756 piastres, raised by public collection and also by the sale of lands belonging to the foundation, despite the written ban on such sales issued by Patriarch Gregory V. The nunnery is coenobite, with forty cells.

The Katholikon (main church) is triform: one of its side chapels being dedicated to St. Pantaleimon and the other to Our Lady as the Source of Life (Zoodochos Piyi). The central church is dedicated to St. Nicholas. Note the fine wooden screen in the Katholikon and the Byzantine icon of St. Nicholas (date unknown). At one time the convent owned over 70 acres of land.

In 1834, a Royal Decree was issued ordering the dissolution of all monasteries with less than 6 monks. Of the approximately 500 monasteries and convents in free Greece at that time, 412 closed down. Only three nunneries remained: that at Kaisariani in Athens, Loukous in Kynouria and that of St. Nicholas on Santorini, which had some 18 nuns at the time. The number soon grew, with the addition of nuns from convents which had closed down.

Weaving was the main occupation of the nuns. The goods they produced were of high quality and fetched good prices. The nuns must also have devoted a good deal of time to the maintenance, care and cleanliness of the convent, which continues to be impressive from that point of view even today.

2.0 km. Imerovigli (otherwise Merovigli or Merevili). The name presumbly comes from the days of piracy, and means the day-time look-out post. The site of the village, more or less in the centre of the caldera and at its highest point, would indeed have permitted watch being kept over the whole area and thus the timely warning of the islanders should pirates appear. The main interest of

The grandeur of Skaros.

the village today lies in its proximity to Skaros. The church, Our Lady 'Malteza', takes its name from the icon around which it centres and which is reputed to have been found in the sea off Malta. As we pass through the village in the direction of the caldera, we will encounter the path to Skaros.

Skaros was once among the five most important settlements on the island (see p. 16). Very few traces of that town now remain. One of the most exciting walks the island has to offer is that which leads, on Skaros, along the path which runs initially S and then W to the 'Theoskepasti' chapel. This dazzlingly white little building, apparently growing out of the rock, commands the abyss from on high. We stand at the most awe-inspiring point on the island, and the view is unparalleled. The walk takes at least an hour, there and back, and should not be attempted by those who suffer from vertigo.

On the way to Oia one can see the strips of earth which centuries of toil have built stone walls to retain.

We return to Imerovigli square and continue towards Oia.

2.3 km. To the right, a road to the village of Vourvoulos, through which we shall pass on the way back.

3.2. km. Left: Imerovigli cemetery.

3.6 km. Left: a small path with a view over the caldera and towards Oia. From this point on and until the 9th km we shall encounter, to the right and left, a number of paths and lanes of no particular interest.

9.0 km. To the right and parallel to the road, the village of **Finikia** which, with **Perivolos** and **Oia**, constitute the island's most northerly settlement. The overall name for the region is **Apano Meria** ('the upper part').

10.05 km. Left: a road to Perivolos.

10.1 km. A fork right, towards Finikia. This road runs almost parallel to that which we are on, but in the opposite direction, given that we are nearly through the village and it lies behind us. A little after this fork, another intersection, to the E, leads to the eastern side of the island

at Baxedes, through which we shall be passing on the way back (see below, km. 14.0).

11.0 km. Fork to the right. This is the start of the road to the NE coast of the island. This is the road we shall be taking back to Fira.

11.2 km. Oia. Left, the square, which is the bus terminal. Other forms of transport can continue until km. 11.7, the centre of Oia. The poor track which turns right just before this leads to the northernmost point of Santorini and almost down to **Ammoudi beach**. The road ends at km. 12.7.

Oia is the second most important town on Santorini, and, for many, its most beautiful spot. The name is very ancient. During the period of 'Frankish' rule Oia was among the five largest settlements. After liberation from the Turks, the inhabitants of Apano Meria developed into leading seafarers. As they grew richer, they invested their wealth in the mansion houses (most of them two-storey) which stand on the upper level of the village. They give the village a personality of its own, not least because they are all painted. The walls are ochre, and the door and window-frames are built in red limestone, as are the little stones used for decoration on the outer walls.

Oia is the island's second-largest resort area, and for many its most beautiful spot.

A figurehead from the Maritime Museum

Among other remains of Oia's seafaring past is its interesting **marine museum**, preserving memories of the glories of the past.

Yet none of this can really explain the fascination which Oia holds for so many people. Perhaps the explanation lies more in the fact that although it is often crowded, Oia is not nearly such a worldly place as Fira. There are none of the nightclubs, discotheques, expensive shops and jewellers which can get in between the visitor and nature. Then there is the sea, which is much more accessible.

The Maritime Museum preserves memories of a glorious past.

The chapel of St. Nicholas on its rock.

There are two paths with steps, one running down the precipice to **Armeni beach** with its little chapel of St. Nicholas on the rock, and the other going to **Ammoudi** beach. There are, too, the NTOG hostels, old 'skafta' which have been restored in the traditional style and which bring all the village's picturesqueness to life. Perhaps all these are part of its charm; but perhaps there is also something else, something intangible. Anyway, Oia is the sort of place that makes you very sensitive to poetry.

The little harbour of Oia from above.

Return Journey. The road starts at the intersection we have already noted, at km. 11.0, and leads E.

12. km. Left: the spot is known as **Tholos** — just a suspicion of a village, with two or three houses.

12.7 km. The road turns right, to the S, and follows the eastern coast of the island.

13.6 km. Fork to the right. We keep straight on.

14.0 km. Baxedes. Fork right for Finikia (see above, km 10.5). Those who decide to return via Finikia will have to turn right once more at km 15.1, and then follow their noses — the road, however, is poor.

15.5. km. Intersection, the left branch of which leads to the beach.

16.7 km. We are now on a height — the peak of a cape, known as **Koloumbos**. In the sea nearby, at a depth of 18.5 metres, is the crater of the same name, which is that of the second volcano of Santorini — the one which erupted in 1650 (see decription on page 20).

17.4 km. A turning right (and another at 17.6 km) lead to the church of St. George "Get-you-out-of-debt". The name is supposedly due to the vow made by a certain member of the faithful that if St. George would intervene to help him pay his debts he, in his turn, would build the saint a church. One wonders what kind of debts the man must have had if this represents the saint's share!

17.9 km. Turning left for the beach.

18.0 km. A turning right for **Pori** and the large church of Our Lady 'tou Kalou'.

19.9 km. Turning left for the beach.

20.1 km. Turning right — the road leads to Imerovigli.

20.2 km. Turning left fo the beach.

20.3 km. Right, church of St. Artemios.

21.1 km. Left, church of St. Irene.

21.7 km. Intersection. The road left leads to Vourvoulos beach. We shall bear right, for the **village of Vourvoulos**. The main point of interest about this settlement is that is has a speciality: it is almost exclusively where the island's muleteers live and where they have their *'estates'*. We follow the road through the village, and turn S.

23.6 km. Intersection: the left-hand branch leads to the Kontochori beach known as **Apoxo Yialos** or **Pigadia** (springs). The reason for this name is easy, for there are springs there although their water is brackish. There are also ruins of a tomato canning plant. We bear right.

24.0 km. Kontochori. Now we are almost back to Fira, of which Kontochori is the eastern quarter. It lies in a hollow, off the main roads, and it is easy not to notice it at all. There are nonetheless two large mansions in it: those of the Dargentas and Kovaios families. They can be admired from outside.

24.5 km. Fira square: end of the route.

ROUTE 4

Fira - Pyrgos - Profitis Ilias

Fira - Pyrgos - Exo Gonia - Profitis Ilias 12.2 km via the main Fira-Perissa road; 9.4 km by the route described here. A visit to Exo Gonia adds 4 km to the total.

To get from Fira to Pyrgos, we can follow the Perissa road as far as km 6.8 (see route 7).

The route proposed here involves a fairly smooth track for some distance (3 km) but it is shorter and has other points of interest.

The fields besides the road appear to be used for growing baskets. In fact they are vines, coiled in this unusual manner for protection from the wind.

In order to reach our starting-point it will be necessary, in view of the one-way system, to go round in a small circle: from Fira square we take the road downhill to the right and at the end of the street we go right again and are on the road which takes us to the southern part of the island. At the first intersection we go right once more, uphill, though instead of turning right for the square we take the track on the left, which leads south but does not pass through the villages.

0.0 km. This is the old road which the muleteers used when going to Pyrgos with their animals. It is more or less straight and today serves the pozzolana quarries.

0.65 km. To the right, a turning for the quarries. They can be seen best from the sea, either on one's journey in by ship, in which case one passes in front of them before docking at Athinios, or on one's way to the volcano by small boat.

1.5 km. Left, a turning for Messaria (see route 7).

3.0. km. We meet the Fira-Perissa road and take it in the direction of Perissa. We are now at km 5.7 of this road (see route 7).

6.8 km. Turning left for Pyrgos, which we take. 50 m, right — a petrol station.

7.4 km. Turning, left, for **Exo Gonia**. This is a little settlement of 100 souls clinging to the side of the mountain and 2 km from the main road. The size of its church, to St. Haralambos, is out of all proportion to the size of the village. The hill on which it towers commands a view over almost the entire island. The interior of the church is entirdy covered with murals, the work of Christoforos Asimis.

This road continues SE, passing through Mesa Gonia (Episkopi) before joining the Kamari road. We will be meet this road again in route 6.

We return to the main road.

7.5 km. The village of Pyrgos.

7.9 km. Pyrgos square

Pyrgos is the village which best preserves its medieval heritage.

Pyrgos (population about 450) is the village in which the character of the medieval communities of Santorini is best preserved (there were four more of these communities: Oia, Skaros, Emboreio and Akrotiri — see p. 18). Built on a hilltop and far from the sea, it was surrounded by a wall whose ruins can still be seen in the village. At a later date the dangers with which the Middle Ages were fraught vanished, and houses began to be built outside the wall, with the village taking the shape it has today. The castle has survived in the walls and in the name of the village, which means 'tower' or 'castle'.

Pyrgos has an incredible number of churches, some of which are quite old. The oldest of all is that of the Dormition of the Virgin ('Theotokaki', locally), built in the 11th century a little after that at Episkopi Gonia.

From the period 1537-1650 we have the churches of the Transformation of the Saviour ('Christoulaki', locally), St. John the Divine, St. Theodosia and the semi-subterranean St. Nicholas 'Kisiras'. The church of the Dedication of the Virgin was built between 1650 and 1664; St. Catherine in 1660, St. George in 1680, St. Demetrios and the Archangel Michael in 1690, St. Nicholas in 1700... and that is far from a complete list. The number does, however, cease to be quite so amazing when one thinks that the island has a total of 352 churches.

All the necessary tourist facilities are to be found in Pyrgos: hostels, rented rooms, restaurants, a doctor, and so on. The village has the further advantage of being close to Perissa and Kamari.

From Pyrgos square we take the surfaced road which runs uphill to the Monastery of the Prophet Elijah (Profitis Ilias). Those who like strenuous exercise may prefer to take the old path, with its steps.

We are climbing up to the highest point on the island. The landscape changes continously, depending on the direction in which the road is running, and the view out over the caldera is most majestic. The crystalline outcrops of rock remind us that this is not only the highest point on the island, but also its oldest, one of the very few which were there before the volcano (see p. 12). The road has a length of 4.2 km.

On the way to service in the Church of Christ, Pyrgos.

The monastery courtyard. In the foreground a font of whitish marble.

12.1 km.: End of the route: the Monastery of the Prophet Elijah (altitude 567 m).

The monastery of the **Prophet Elijah** was built in the early 18th century (1711-1724) and was originally smaller than the complex of buildings we see today. The extension was made a hundred years later, in the mid-19th century, when King Othon, first king of modern Greece, visited the monastery, was enchanted by the site and judged that it was worth the effort of expanding the foundation.

In its original form the monastery was coenobite, with strict regulations, and until 1853 entry was entirely forbidden to women. Nowadays the number of monks has dropped to so low a level that the term 'coenobite' has very little meaning. The monastery was rich, both in land and in intellectual activity. Until 1931 it had some 400 acres of vineyards, reduced today to 90 after three successive rounds of expropriation. The most notable achievement in the field of learning was the school run by the monastery in Pyrgos from the last days of Turkish rule (1806) until 1845.

The church is visited first, and then the museum, which consists of two collections, one ecclesiastical and the other of folk art. The church museum contains all the monastery's holy objects: Cretan icons of the 15th century and folk icons of the 18th; holy vessels, crucifixes, chalices, holy relics, vestuments —including the mitre of Patriarch Gregory V— manuscript codices of the 8th century, Patriarchal seals and epistles and Turkish firmans granting privileges to the monastery. Apart from more modern works, the library contains 1200 old books, chiefly religious in content.

The folk museum is housed in the part of the monastery in which the monks did their domestic chores. All the fittings, with traditional furniture and equipment, have been left in place, and it is easy for the visitor to imagine what the daily round of toil for islanders of the last century must have been like. The monastery also houses the private collection of P. Nomikos, containing woven goods, embroidery, china and paintings from old mansions.

The monastery gatehouse, under the belfry.

A room in the folklore museum.

The ornate wooden screen from the main church, the work of Demis Langadas (1836).

For those who are fond of tough walking, a path begins at the monastery and leads east to Mesa Vouno; from there it forks, one branch leading to Perissa and the other to Kamari. Stout laced shoes are necessary, for one's feet sink into the eroded ground and walking becomes very difficult when your shoes are full of earth.

ROUTE 5

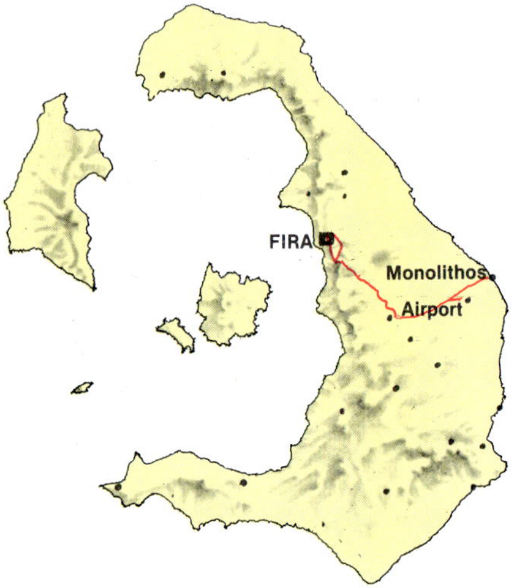

Fira - Monolithos - Airport

Fira - Monolithos (harbour): 7.7 km
Fira - Airport: 5.8 km
Total route (with deviations, possible further routes and return to Fira): 21 km.

The purpose of this itinerary is largely to go swimming. The Monolithos beach is the most suitable on the island for small children and those who are not strong swimmers.

The Limani beach, at Monolithos.

Monolithos with the white church of St. John in a recess.

0.0 km. From Fira we take the road leading to the southern part of the island, as in the previous route, and continue until the Messaria crossroads.

3.4 km. Messaria: we turn left.

4.0 km. Right, turning for Kamari (see route 6). We continue straight on.

4.6 km. Turning half-left. This leads to Monolithos along a narrow track without passing the airport. There is no particular reason to go this way unless we are in a tearing hurry.

5.5 km. Turning left for Monolithos. The road continues straight ahead for a further 300 m before ending at the **Airport** (5.8 km). We turn left.

6.0 km. Turning right for the sea. This is the point at which the narrow track to Monolithos which we encountered at km 4.6 ends.

7.0 km. Our road ends at a three-way crossroads. Directly in front of us is the **rock of Monolithos** —from which the region gets its name— with the white church of St. John in a niche. Monolithos is another remnant of Aegeis, like Mesa Vouno at Perissa (see route 7, and p. 109). This means that before the volcano erupted it must have been a reef surrounded by sea.

We take the left-hand turning.

7.7 km. Now we are at the beach named **Limani**. (In the past, this name was used to describe the whole area, but Monolithos has taken its place today). The two quays which enclose it explain the name (which means 'harbour') and are evidence of efforts at some time in the past to build a port here for Santorini. The location is entirely unsuitable for this, of course, because it is quite unsheltered from the wind and because the sea-bed is shallow and sandy. Thus the site was never used as a harbour. The beach, though, provides good swimming, particularly for those who merely paddle, since there is fine black sand and the sea is shallow until quite a long way out.

To our left, an abandoned tomato-processing factory.

8.1 km. Another tomato factory, this time belonging to the Co-operative. This is the only one in operation on Santorini, under the conditions we have described on p. 38. Its products (tomato puree, tinned tomatoes and tomato juice) are of incomparable taste, precisely because of the quality of the raw materials. They can be bought from the Co-operative's shop in Fira.

The beach near Karterados.

8.4 km. End of the road. All there is from here on is a sandy expanse along the top of the beach which it would be unwise to attempt by car. Walking along it will at length bring us to Exo Yialos, below Karterados (see route 7).

We return to the Mololithos crossroads, from which we can take the branch which leads to the south (returning, that is, to km 7.0).

7.0 km. This road leads south parallel to the airport runway, between it and the sea. The walk along here is of interest only to those who want to be able to say that they have been everywhere.

7.6 km. Left, tracks running down to the sea.

7.9 km. Left, another track to the sea (300 m).

8.2 km. Right, a chapel of St. Paraskeve, imprisoned by fences and barbed wire within the airport perimeter.

8.3 km. Left, a track to the sea.

8.9 km. Left, a track to an abandoned tomato factory.

9.1 km. End of the road and of the route. A little further along in front of us are the ruins of yet another tomato factory.

Beyond this Kamari beach begins, but this is reached by another road (see route 6).

ROUTE 6

Fira - Kamari - Mesa Vouno

Fira - Mesa Vouno: 10.9 km
Total itinerary, with deviations: 25.2 km

Route: Fira - Messaria - Mesa Gonia - Kamari - Mesa Vouno - Kamari - Return.

The objectives of this route are to visit a Byzantine monument, to visit ancient Thera and have lunch and a swim at Kamari beach. The visits should be allowed one and a half to two hours. To give oneself plenty of time, one should count on leaving in the morning and returning in the late afternoon.

We may come here for a swim, but not by donkey; its day has passed.

Our Lady Episkopi Gonia (facade).

0.0 km. The first part of this route is the same as the start of route 5, which we follow up to km 4.

4.0 km. Turning for Kamari. We bear right.

4.75 km. Turning right for Vothonas (no road sign). We pass by.

5.65 km. The road on our right is the end of the road from Pyrgos through Exo Gonia (see route 4).

5.7 km. The road on our right (and those at kms. 5.9 and 5.95) leads to Mesa Gonia. We pass it, arriving at

6.2 km. at which point we encounter the main road to Mesa Gonia. We follow this for 1.1 km. At the start of the road the village of **Mesa Gonia** or **Episkopis Gonia** is right in front of us, an impressive collection of collapsing houses and general abandonment. There are only 75 inhabitants, yet this is one of the villages in which most stock-breeding is done.

After 400 m we reach the entrance to the village and turn left. We go on for a further 700 m before reaching the courtyard of the most important Byzantine monument on Santorini, the *"Piskopi Gonia"* church, built in the 11th century.

Episkopi Gonia today is nothing but a pretty little chapel with interesting architecture. Once, however, it was a place of great importance and it gave rise to many years of conflict between Orthodox and Catholic.

Our Lady of Gonia, dedicated to the Dormition of the Virgin, seems to have been founded by the Emperor Alexios Comnenus (1081-118) and to have been the seat of the Bishop of Santorini. However, when in 1207 the Franks arrived, the church was turned over to the Catholics. In 1537, when the Turks conquered the island, the Orthodox population exploited the opportunity to get part of it back. The church estates were shared out between the Orthodox and Catholic flocks, and both had the right to use the church for worship. That was when the disputes began: who would be the first to hold their service on August 15 (feast of Our Lady), and who would be the first to celebrate Vespers on the previous day? These disputes sometimes involved a resort to arms. In 1768 the Patriarch and the Sultan combined to put a stop to the quarrel by banning the Catholics from the church altogether. When the modern Greek state was formed, the church property was gradually appropriated, and all that is left of it today is the site of the church and its surrounding court.

The building we see today is not exactly that which was put up in the 11th century. Minor additions have been made from time to time, among which are the bell tower and the outside staircase. The details of the building have also disappeared, since unfortunately at some point it was plastered and whitewashed, its red roof-tiles not excepted! What has remained untouched is the carved screen inside, of blue marble with a white grain. The limestone block in the courtyard with the indentation and hole is reputed to be the sacrificial altar of an ancient temple. The hole was for the blood to run out. The church was robbed some years ago and all its vaduable icons stolen. There are traces of wall-paintings.

We return to our road at km. 6.2.

6.7 km. The track leading off to the right goes to a quarry (700 m). We pass by.

7.4 km. Now we are at Kamari. To our left, a road to the beach which we ignore.

7.6 km. The road widens into a sort of square where the buses park; it does go on a little further, however.

7.9 km. To our left, the main beach road (300 m).

In ancient times **Kamari** was the port for Thera (which we shall soon be visiting, at Mesa Vouno) and was called Oia. Today it is a coastal settlement which has literally grown from nothing and has developed at an amazing rate. On p. 34-35 we have already described what the area was like before the earthquakes: it was simply a place, and there were no houses here. Now it is a large village

Kamari from Mesa Vouno.

of some 600 inhabitants, which grows larger and more developed every year.

Kamari owes this burst of development to its sea and its beach. It should be remembered that many visitors seek to find in Santorini what they can find on other islands: the sun, the sea and the sand. This is the best place for that: there is a long east-facing beach, with coarse black sand, and the south end of the beach is protected by the perpendicular mass of Mesa Vouno. The water is crystal-clear. The only thing to be careful of is that the sea rapidly becomes very deep, much more quickly than one might expect on a sandy beach, and that there are strong cross-currents which may form dangerous whirlpools. Another advantage of Kamari, and one which makes it almost unique for Santorini, is that there are undrground sources of water.

More or less anything one could possibly want is to be found at Kamari: a large hotel with a swimming-pool, rooms for rent, hosts of restaurants, fish tavernas, a cinema, discotheques, and space to put up tents. It is a pity, though, that the beach itself cannot be made any bigger; for how much longer, one wonders, will it be able to cope with the demand?

Despite the attractions of the beach, we would do well to go up to Mesa Vouno. Swimming will be even more pleasant by the time we have finished. We return to the point at

which we left the main road (7.9 km) and continue towards Mesa Vouno. The road winds up the rocky mass with narrow hairpin bends, although the road is quite passable. The climb is 3 km long and is so steep that Kamari is soon visible below rather as if we were seeing it from an aeroplane. To the right of our road, on the side of the hill, can be seen the old road, which climbed the hill with steps.

10.9 km. We reach a piece of flat ground 264 m above sea level, this being the saddle between the main hill crowned by the Prophet Elijah monastery and a second, lower, hill to the east named **Mesa Vouno**. Ancient Thera is on the western side of Mesa Vouno — right in front of us, that is. The saddle on which we stand is called **Sellada**. Looking towards the entrance to the archaeological site, we have on our right the start of the path to Perissa, which we can see from above. On our left is Kamari and the road by which we came. Behind us is a path leading up to the Prophet Elijah. (see route 4).

The black sand and the cold, clear water make a swim at Kamari an unforgettable experience.

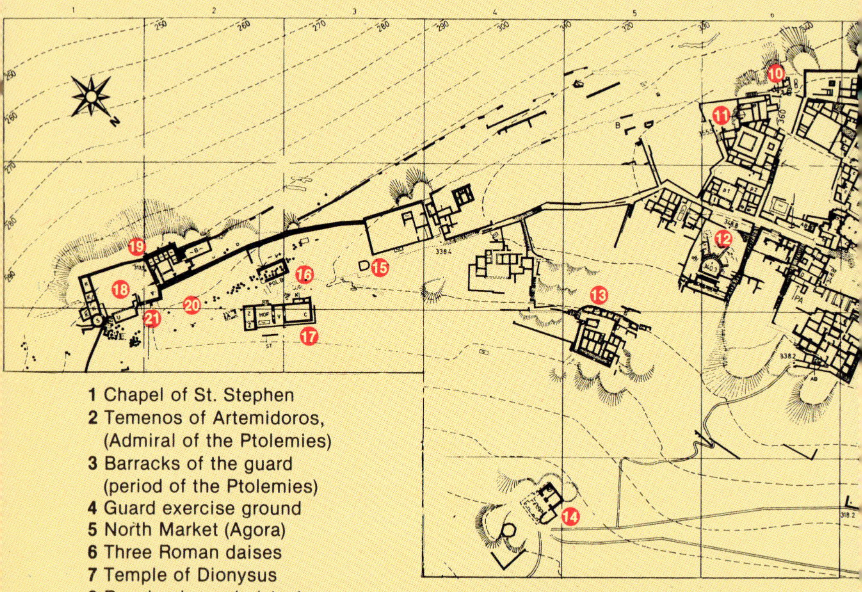

1 Chapel of St. Stephen
2 Temenos of Artemidoros, (Admiral of the Ptolemies)
3 Barracks of the guard (period of the Ptolemies)
4 Guard exercise ground
5 North Market (Agora)
6 Three Roman daises
7 Temple of Dionysus
8 Royal colonnade (stoa)
9 The house with phallus
10 Sanctuary of the Egyptian deities
11 Temple of Pythian Apollo (later a Byzantine church)
12 Theatre
13 Roman baths
14 Chapel of the Annunciation
15 Sanctuary of Ptolemy III Euergetes
16 Column of Artemis

Ancient Thera is a long and narrow settlement (800 m by 150 m), running NW-SE, with an average altitude of 350 m, and crossed by one main street along its long axis, intersected by numerous side streets. We begin our visit at the NW corner and walk SE. The excavations were were conducted, as we have already said (see route 1, the Fira Museum), by Baron von Goertringen between 1896 and 1900; the finds show that Dorian colonists inhabited the area as early as the 9th century BC, and that during the Hellenistic period (300-145 BC) the Ptolemies had a strong garrison here, right above the island's principal harbour, Oia, which we know as Kamari today. In other words, in the 4th century BC Kamari and Mesa Vouno were an Egyptian naval base. There are Byzantine remains, too, at Mesa Vouno.

The first remains we shall encounter on entering the archaeological site are Byzantine, too. They lie beneath the chapel of St. Stephen and are of a 4th or 5th century basilica dedicated to the Archangel Michael.

We continue along the path. About 200 metres further along, to our right, we come to the Temenos (sacred precinct) of Artemodorus, admiral of the Ptolemies, with inscriptions, the symbols of various gods (Zeus, Apollo, Poseidon) and dedications to others (Priapus and Hecate

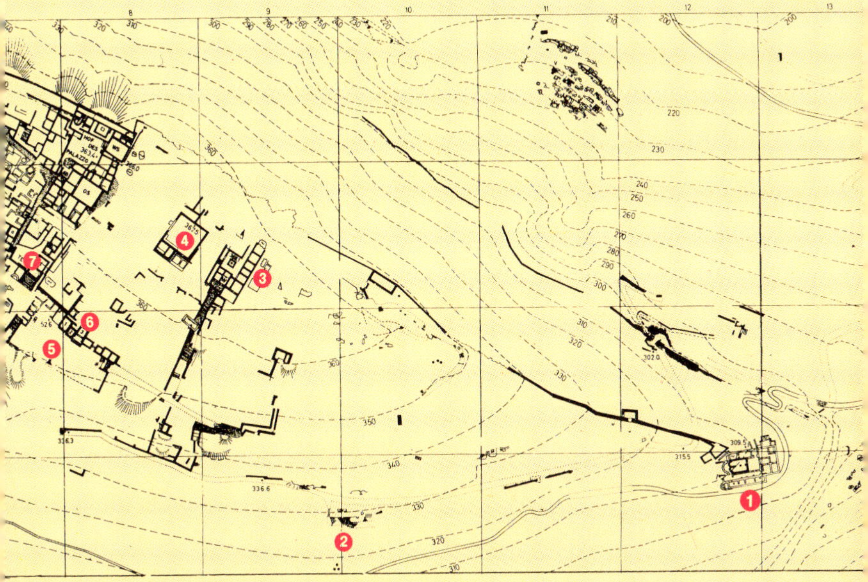

17 Temple of Carneian Apollo
18 Training-ground of the ephebes
19 Baths of the ephebes
20 Terrace of the dancing
21 Cave of Hermes and Heracles

Map of Ancient Thera

among them). A hundred or so metres further on, to the right, a path with steps climbs up to the barracks of the garrison of the Ptolemies. To the left of the barracks was the Gymnasium of the garrison.

Continuing along the main path, we come to a wider part on the left which was the Agora (market-place), 110 metres long by 17-30 metres broad. We are at its northern end and as we walk along we shall see three Roman Exedres, or daises. Immediately after these, on the right again, is the temple of Dionysus, to which a series of steps lead. Now we are in the central portion of the Agora, and we walk towards the southern part which, on its left on the downward slope, has a group of houses and on its right the Royal Stoa, with a colonnade along its main axis. The dimensions are 41.5 metres by 10.1 metres. Immediately behind the colonnade is the house with the phallus and the inscription ΤΟΙΣ ΦΙΛΟΙΣ (to my friends). A larger group of houses extends behind and slightly above the colonnade.

The Sacred Way starts in the southern corner of the Agora and leads south. As soon as we enter upon it we have on our right a large rectangular area like a square. A little beyond the SW corner of this square was the sanctuary of Isis, Serapis and Anubis; to the left of this was the temple of Pythian Apollo, on which a Byzantine church was later built.

The house of the phallus

We continue along the Sacred Way. To our left is the theatre, as converted by the Romans. Behind it and a little to the south are baths, also dating from Roman times. Even further over, on the downward slope, we can see the chapel of the Annunciation.

After a short while the Sacred Way disappears and becomes a path once more. We come, in sequence, to the sanctuary of Ptolemy III Euergetes (the Benefactor), the Column of Artemis, the temple of Apollo Karneios, and the Gymnasium of the Ephebes (adolescent boys) with baths and its training ground. To the left of the Gymnasium is the cave of Hermes and Herakles.

This is where our visit to the archaeological site ends, and we can now go back to Kamari for the swim and the meal which we undoubtedly deserve.

Reliefs at the te

Ancient Thera today.

of Artemidoros.

Roman Theatre

ROUTE 7

Fira - Perissa

Main route: Fira - Messaria - Vothonas - Megalochori - Emboreio - Perissa (14 km). (Perivolos - Ai Yiorgis -Oxomytis - Vlychada: 16.9 km).

Secondary routes:
a) Karterados - Yialos Karteradou (2.5 km).
b) Athinios (11.1 km).

All the routes we suggest above end at one beach or another, and so this is a day's outing to be combined with a swim. The main route ends on the southern beaches, the first secondary route on the east coast and the second on the west. Thus the beach from which one is going to swim can be chosen on the basis of the direction of the wind.

Vothonas and Messaria from our route.

Main Route

0.0 km. From the Fira square, we take the road with the eucalyptus trees. This is the southern part of Santorini's main road, which ends at Perissa after passing —directly or by means of side-roads— through most of the villages on the island.

0.5 km. Right: one of the two petrol stations of which Santorini can boast. The other is at the entrance to the village of Pyrgos, in the same direction, 7 km further along (see route 4).

1.1 km. Left: turning for Karterados. We continue straight on.

1.3 km. Left: second turning for Karterados, immediately after a little chapel (see below, secondary route a).

1.7 km. Left: a cobbled pathway also leading to Karterados.

3.4 km. Intersection. The left branch leads towards Monolithos, airport and Kamari, see route 5. The right branch takes us to Messaria, which is 300 m away, and whose centre can be entered by turning right once again.

Messaria is a lively inland village with about 400 inhabitants. It stands at the crossroads of the island's main roads, and, despite its distance from the coast, this is enough to explain the number of small hotels, bars and so on which are to be seen as one enters the village. Messaria is primarily agricultural. Its co-operative was one of the island's most active, and even today Messaria produces a major proportion of the Santorini wine.

What really proves the vigour of the villagers of Messaria is their eye clinic, founded in 1929. At the beginning of this century some 80% of the island's inhabitants suffered from trachoma (chronic contagious conjunctivitis) which leads to blindness. It was three ordinary men from Messaria who undertook the fight against this scourge: Michail Danezis, Vasileios Nomikos and Emmanouil Gavrilis. The first of these three provided the inspirition and the other two the capital. More locals joined in, and the St. Barbara Eye Clinic of Thera was founded in Messaria. By 1948, the incidence of trachoma had falled to 19%. In 1954, the state closed down the clinic because it was under private law.

We continue, in the direction of Pyrgos. The road begins to run uphill, and there are frequent bends.

Directly after the first intersection is the village of **Vothonas**, with a population of 300. In appearance, it resembles a continuation of Messaria on the other side of the road.

3.9 km. Right, an intersection with a road leading back to Messaria.

If the time of year is one at which the vines happen to be in leaf, it is worth stopping for a moment on our way up the hill, in order to see the crafty way which the islanders have found to protect their crop from the wind. Each vine plant is pruned in such a way as to form one huge stem, which is then trained to grow in coils round and round its root, just as one might coil a hose. When the vine is in leaf, the new twigs emerge from the coil and bear their fruit, but only a relatively small area of the surface of the vine itself is exposed to the wind.

In the winter, it looks from a distance as if the whole plain is scattered with woven baskets.

5.7 km. Right, another side road. This is an unsurfaced track leading straight from Fira and clearly something of a short-cut (see route 4).

6.8 km. Intersection: now we are at the top of the hill. To the right, a chapel of St. Andrew. To the left, the road to Pyrgos (see route 4).

7.7 km. Right, turning to Athinios: see below, secondary route b. From here, the road runs down gently to the southern plain.

8.5 km. Left, turning to **Megalochori** (population 250).

10.2 km. Right, turning to Akrotiri and the archaeological site (see route 8).

11.7 km. Right, turning for Vlychada, see below, after Perissa.

12.1 km. We pass through the village of **Emboreio** or Nimborio. This is the largest village in the south of the island, standing in the midst of the plain of the same name, and is picturesque, with narrow alleyways, old neighbourhoods and a population of about a thousand. The name of the village (it is related to the English word 'emporium') and the ruined windmills which can be seen on the hill opposite bear witness to its commercial activities in the past. What is not perhaps evident at a first glance is that the villagers also engage in fishing. Perissa is their home port and they keep their boats there. Once the village had its own alarm service, known as the lantern man, who got up before dawn and went from house

The 'goulas' (fortified mansion) at Emborio, one of the surviving medieval fortresses.

Emborio or Nimborio.

to house rousing the fishermen.

Under the Venetians, the village had one of the island's five castles and also a fortified mansion (goulas). Ruins have survived.

12.2 km. Right, turning to the beach of St. George (Ai Yiorgis) "the Seafarer" ('Thalassinos').

13.3 km. Right, turning to Perivolos beach.

15.0 km. Perissa. Now we are at the end of our route. There are three main elements in the view we see before us: first the fine black sand of the beach. Second the stony mass of Mesa Vouno rising almost perpendicularly at the eastern end of the beach and which has nothing in common with the type of stone to which Santorini has so far accustomed us. This is one of the peaks of ancient Aegeis which remained above the surface of the sea when the Aegean was formed and consequently was there before the volcano erupted and before Santorini came into being (see also p. 10). Third and last, there is the Perissa church, dedicated to the Holy Cross, which is a place of pilgrimage for the islanders. The church, which is the largest on Santorini, comes as something of a surprise, seemingly rising out of the sand at a spot where one would expect at most a little chapel.

Not that Perissa does not have a chapel, too: that of St. Irene, dating from the late 16th or early 17th century, and claimed by many to be the origin of the name of the island. This claim is, however, disputed —and

Perissa. Some of the best swimming on the island is to be had her

the shelter of the enormous rock of Mesa Vouno.

The southern beach extends westwards almost all the way along the cape.

perhaps with some justice— by St. Irene on Thirasia (see route 2).

The beach of Perissa is one of the two most frequented on the island. It has all the necessary facilities, restaurants, refreshment stands, etc.

The south coast of the island, beginning to the east at Mesa Vouno, runs west almost right along to Akrotiri, frequently changing names. After Perissa is the Perivolos beach; this is followed by Ai Yiorgis Thalassinos, Oxomytis and Vlychada. The other beaches, lying still further west, are reached from other roads and are not covered by this itinerary. They are all fine beaches, and much less crowded. They cannot be reached directly from Perissa; access is via the side roads we encountered on our way from Emboreio. So we returne:

The turning at 13.3 km leads to **Perivolos** (1 km).

The turning at 12.2 km leads first to **Ai Yiorgis** beach (14 km) and from there runs almost along the edge of the sea, westwards to **Oxomytis** and **Vlychada** (16.9 km).

Vlychada can also be reached from the turning at 11.7 km. by taking the road which in the beginning runs W and then turns S.

The roads running from all these turnings are passable unsurfaced tracks. There are impressive ruined tomato canning factories on the beaches.

Secondary Routes

A. Fira - Karterados - Yialos Karteradou (2.5 km)

From Fira, we follow the main route until km 1.3, the second turning to Karterados, where we bear left. The road —a good track— leads to the southern part of the island, crossing it at one point.

Karterados (population 570) is most striking for its position. Once one has got used to the landscape of Santorini, with its villages usually erected at commanding points, Karterados, built in a gulley with its roofs on the same level as the road, comes as a considerable surprise. Of course, its position protects it against the north winds, which pass right over the top of it, given that the gulley runs from east to west. Another reason for its position may be that the gulley provides two almost vertical banks which are ideal for the construction of 'skafta' houses in the otherwise almost flat landscape around the village.

After passing the square, one can stop to observe the three churches on the left. The one in the middle, of the Ascension, is the main village church and is an example of the western style imported from Italy as it was adapted in the Cyclades. The floor plan is that of a Byzantine cross in a square and there is a dome on top, but there are also two tower-like belfries, in front, to the left and right of the main entrance. The colour, too, is indicative of the church's foreign descent: the main exterior surfaces are ochre, with a little white on the mouldings, the windowsills and the door and window frames. The dome is neither the pure azure which was the custom in the island nor white. It is the light bluish-green of tarnished copper, and together with the ochre and the white it makes a fine composition in pastel shades. The church of the Ascension in Karterados is reminiscent of the Cathedral of Fira, Our Lady "Belonia", as it was before the earthquake.

To the right and left of the Ascension, as we see them from the road, are the churches of the Dedication of the Virgin and of St. Nicholas, built in the Santorinian style, providing a sharp contrast with the larger church they flank. They are rectangular basilicas, with semi-circular vaulted roofs, and the front wall extends upwards as a pediment, above the level of the vault, to form a flat triangular 'belfry'. There are three openings in the base of the triangle, rising to semi-circular arches, and a fourth at the point of the triangle, each holding a bell. Naturally, these churches are painted white.

As we leave the village, on the left, there is a tennis court. The sight of the tennis court, so suddenly, with the absolute clarity of its lines and colours in the sandy, almost lunar, landscape, sets one thinking involuntarily of Dali. The tennis court and its surroundings might almost be the subject of a surrealist painting entitled "The Oasis".

About one kilometre from the end of Karterados, we come to **Exo Yialos**, the beach of Karterados. The beach is a good one, with black sand and large pebbles, some tamarisks for shade, a restaurant, showers and for the present at least, very few people. When there is not a north wind, Exo Yialos at Karterados is ideal for swimming, as it is the closest beach to Fira.

B. Fira - Athinios (11.1 km)

From Fira we follow the main route until km 7.7, at which point we encounter a road to the right, in the direction of the caldera, which takes us to **Athinios**, the port of Santorini. The road winds steeply down for 3.4 km and there are many bends. It was built relatively recently and is the only one the island which goes to a point at which a boat can anchor. Its construction was decisive in the modernisation of the island (see also p. 26). The cliff we are descending is, like Mesa Vouno, at Perissa, one of the remnants of Aegeis, with a light-coloured crystalline stone formation different from the familiar volcanic landscape of the island.

When we reach the bottom, at Athinios, we will find a few little houses, a restaurant or two, bars, and, above all, the quay. This is perhaps the most precious thing on the island — its lifeline to the outside world. To the right of the jetty is an attractive little beach with pebbles. One last swim is always the best thing to do while waiting for the boat to appear.

Only here, at Athinios, can boats dock.

ROUTE 8

Fira - Akrotiri

Fira - Akrotiri (archaeological site): 15.2 km.

Total itinerary (as far as the lighthouse and including the return to Fira): 40.6 km.

Our objective in this route is to come to grips with the ancient civilisation of Santorini as it was before the eruption of 1450 BC and the sinking of half the island.

The village of Akrotiri.

For the first 10.2 km of this route we shall follow the Perissa road (see route 7); in other words, we go past the turning for Pyrgos, to the left, and that for Athinios, on our right, and continue for a further 2.5 km. Of course, the part of the route between Fira and Pyrgos can be done via the road referred to in route 4, which is somewhat shorter.

10.1 km. Turning right for Akrotiri. We take this road.

12.8 km. To our left, a chapel. To the right, directly opposite, a track which goes down into the caldera and after about 1000 m encounters the sea.

13.0 km. Another fork to the right. This avoids the village of Akrotiri and, after 5.5 km, reaches the furthest point of the cape, where the light-house stands.

13.2 km. We are at the entrance to the village **Akrotiri**, which was one of the island's five castles during Frankish times. Today there are about two hundred inhabitants, and it would be an isolated spot, lying off the main road axis of the island, if the neighbouring archaeological site did not attract people and trade all year.

After 100 m we turn left and head in the direction of the southern beach.

14.5 km. We are now almost at the beach. The entrance to the archaeological site is on our left.

The **excavations at Akrotiri** started in 1967, under Professor Spyros Marinatos, and their aim was to prove the theory that the destruction of Minoan civilisation in Crete was the result of the eruption of the volcano on Santorini. The dig was most revealing. Apart from confirming the theory, the excavations resulted in the following archaeological conclusions:

— The eruption of the volcano was preceded by earthquakes, and the inhabitants had plenty of time to get organised and abandon their dwellings (no skeletons, human or animal, were found, nor were any objects of value).

— There may have been a period of calm which allowed some of the inhabitants to return and try to repair their halfruined houses (tools had obviously been hurriedly thrown down at various points). They, too, however, had time to leave before the eruption.

— The space of time between earthquake and eruption may have been as much as a year (seeds had the time to sprout before being covered by lava).

— Akrotiri was the site of an organised community with high living standards, possibly governed by a priest caste.

— Nature and Fertility were the objects of religious worship.

— Each house had its own shrine, skilfully decorated with murals, and there was no temple as such.

— The art of the inhabitants of Akrotiri was very similar to Cretan art in the Minoan period.

— No written records were found to allow clearer conclusions to be drawn, but there is con-

The triangular square and the West House.

siderable evidence to support the identification of Strongyle with Atlantis.

We enter the archaeological site, which is unique of its kind. Most of the archaeological sites with which one becomes familiar in Greece (the Acropolis of Athens, Delphi, Olympia, Pella, Dodona, Epidaurus, Mycenae, Knossos) are monuments. They belong to no one. One admires them for their beauty, for the splendour, for their technical perfection, but one's admiration remains outside the life of which they were a part. All these monuments were connected by particular and individual moments or aspects of this life, which in turn were directly linked to the civilisations which had created them. For the few who have studied those civilisations, the monuments become eloquent and sometimes even loquacious witnesses. Perhaps these people can bring the monuments back to life by an effort of the imagination. For the many, however, the monuments remain mute.

The area which we are now entering, on the other hand, is a familiar one: a place for routine, daily life. There are two-and three-storeyed houses, windows, toilets, cookhouses, workshops, lanes, drains, and shops. All this belongs or belonged to people one can easily imagine living there because one can easily imagine oneself living among them. One may even feel as though one were trespassing when entering other people's houses just because the owners have

Part of the ruins; room D2, on the eastern side of sector D.

run away and left them. Then, when one suddenly thinks that these houses were built 3,500 years ago, one does fall to wondering why all the time expressed in that enormous number seems in no way to intrude between us and the houses.

Excavation has uncovered a long and narrow section of the city, running along a N-S axis (see plan of the ancient city). We enter at the S side and head N.

To our left, the first large building we come to, under the protective roof, has been named from its frontage of hewn stone. The ground floor consists of some 10 rooms. An impressive staircase leads to the first floor and there are indications that there must have been a second floor as well. The murals found in this house covered a total wall space of 100 m^2.

We continue north, entering the stone-paved *Telchines Street*. To our left, is House *C*. To our right, the two-storeyed House *B*, in which were found the following wall-paintings: the *Antelopes*, the *Young Boxers*, the *Apes*. The ground floor of *B1* was a storeroom, in which great jars were found in special niches in the walls.

We continue along the right (east) side of the town, leaving House *C* for the return journey. The road broadens and forms a square, known as *Mill Square* from the little rooms which are to be been on its northern

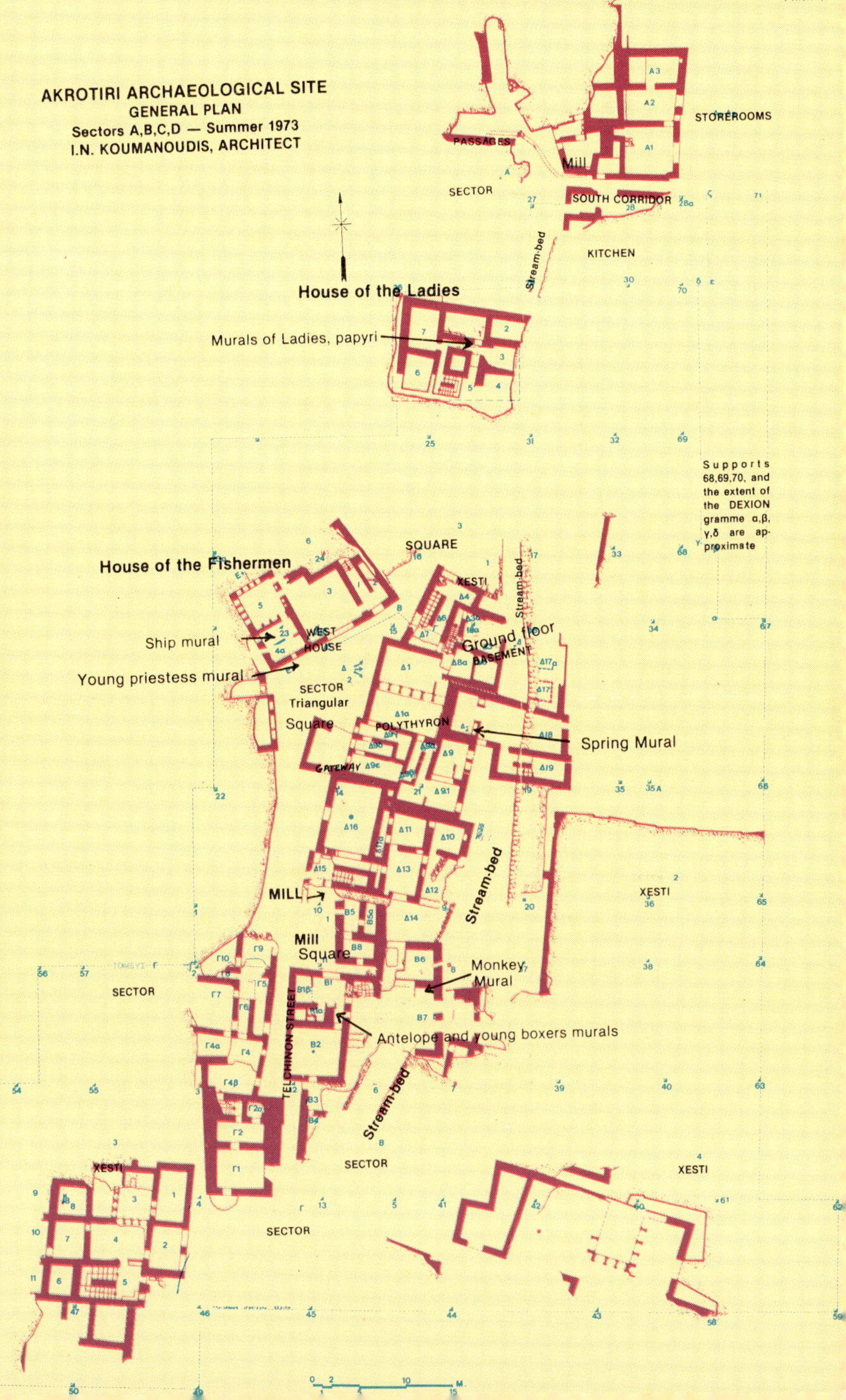
AKROTIRI ARCHAEOLOGICAL SITE
GENERAL PLAN
Sectors A,B,C,D — Summer 1973
I.N. KOUMANOUDIS, ARCHITECT
STOREROOMS
PASSAGES
Mill
SECTOR
SOUTH CORRIDOR
KITCHEN
Stream-bed
House of the Ladies
Murals of Ladies, papyri
Supports 68,69,70, and the extent of the DEXION gramme α,β, γ,δ are approximate
SQUARE
House of the Fishermen
XESTI
WEST HOUSE
Ground floor
BASEMENT
Ship mural
Young priestess mural
SECTOR
Triangular Square
POLYTHYRON
Spring Mural
GATEWAY
MILL
Mill Square
Stream-bed
XESTI
SECTOR
Monkey Mural
TELCHINON STREET
Antelope and young boxers murals
Stream-bed
XESTI
SECTOR
XESTI
SECTOR

side and which were the workshop of a miller. The mill for grinding wheat can still be seen inside, as can the built-in jar into which the flour fell.

The *Mill* is the NW extremity (*D15*) of complex *D*, which lies on our right as we walk on. The western entrance to this complex, under the Propylon, leads to the following areas:

D1: the ground floor of this area, to judge from the utensils and fittings, must have been a kitchen of some kind. The upper floor is very characteristic of Minoan architecture in that it is separated by a raised course of stone.

D2: contained the *Spring* wall-painting — a landscape with lilies among which swallows frolic.

D9: a huge number of pots was found here, as also in

D16: where in addition the pots were arranged according to size, shape and quality. *D16* was probably a shop.

The external wall of *D1* and the house opposite it (the *Western house or House of the Fishermen*) form a triangular square. We cross this heading N. There is another entrance to house *D* on its northern side, behind which a staircase leads to the upper floor.

We now approach the most northerly part of the uncovered area, where stands Building *A*, which must

The spring mural, from room D2 (National Archaeological Museum).

Mural from the House of the Fishermen (National Archaeological Museum).

Mural from the House of the Ladies (National Archaeological Museum).

have been a storehouse. This at least is the conclusion to be drawn from the vast number of pithoi (storage jars) found inside it. In some of the jars were carbonised remains of flour, barley and other foodstuffs. Building A also produced part of a wall-painting whose subject (the head of an African with curly hair, an ear-ring and thick lips) has been found nowhere else in Minoan Cretan art.

After Building *A* we turn S once more, to visit the western part of the city.

First we come, on the right, to the *House of the Ladies*, in which were found murals showing bare-breasted ladies, as in Crete, and others representing papyroi. Apart from pottery, stone tools were also found in this house.

We return to the *Triangular Square*. In its NW corner is the *House of the Fishermen*. In this were found two murals showing *fishermen*, one with a *young priestess* and the famous mural with the *ships*.

We continue S, reaching *Mill Square* again, and enter *Telchines Street*. On our right is Building *C*, in which many stone tools were found.

Note: work on the site continues, and new buildings are being laid bare each year. This tour round the site is in accordace with what was to be seen in 1986. Visitors are conducted round a set route by guides.

Mammary-form water-jug and flower vase (National Archaeological Museum). Below: jars on the site.

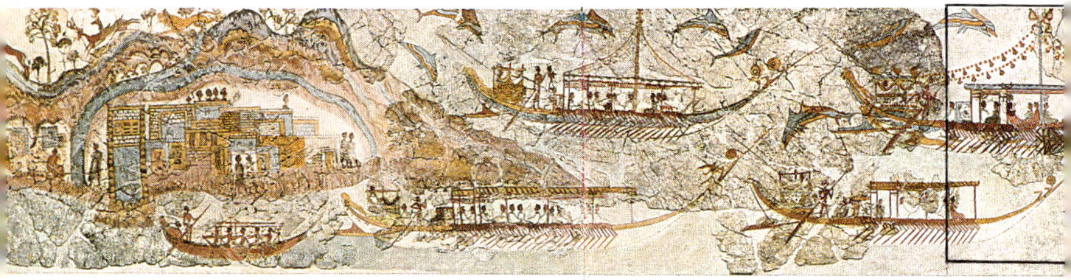

The famous ship mural from the south wall of room 5

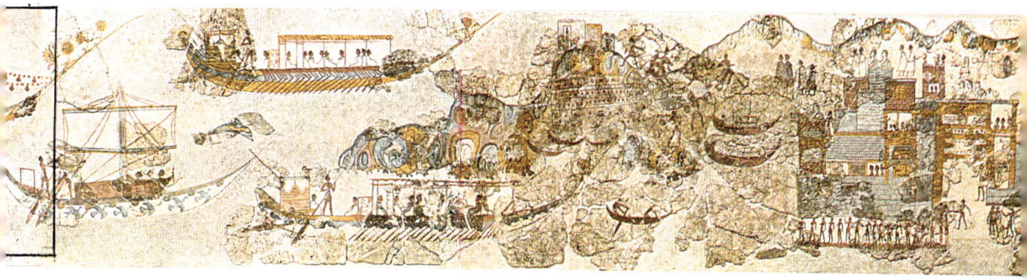

in the West House (National Archaeological Museum).

The young boxers from room B1 (National Archaeological Museum).

The ship mural (detail).

As we leave the archaeological site, we can go straight to the beach which lies some two hundred metres further down, where there is a hotel and a restaurant, but much better swimming is to be found further along: a track starts exactly opposite the entrance to the archaeological site and leads W, running more or less along the line of the coast.

15.2 km. We reach the particularly attractive spot known as **Mavro Rachidi**. It stands out for its black and reddish rocks which run down to the sea and for the chapel of St. Nicholas which strikes a contrast, with its dazzling white, against the dark background of the rocks.

We leave our transport here.

Crossing the chapel courtyard, we take the path which after some 400 metres, brings us to an excellent beach (Kokkini Ammos, or Red Sand). This is the place to swim.

This beach can also be reached by boat from the beach directly after the archaeological site.

Down by the beach is a taverna unlike any other: a cave dug out of the ground. The interior gives some idea of what the houses once felt like. Barba-Nikolas makes sure his wine is made in the true traditional way.

The lighthouse stands at the island's farthest extremity.

We return to the point at which we left the surfaced road, at km 13 of our route.

After 200 m, on the left of the road we have taken, is the village we have skirted, and to our right the caldera sea.

14.1 km. Turning, left. The track leads to the western entrance to Akrotiri.

14.5 km. To the left, right on the bend, the chapel of St. John.

14.8 km. To the left, turning for the Church of Our Lady. From there there is a minor road leading to St. John's chapel.

14.9 km. Another turning left. The track leads S and itself forks after a further 100 m. If we go straight on, we will come, in 1000 m, to the underground church of the Archangel. If we take the fork, we shall come out either at the church of Our Lady (front left) or at that of Christ (to our right after 1 km).

16.3 km. Left, a track for **Mesa Pigadi**, the southern beach of the cape (about 1 km).

17.6 km. Right, another track to the caldera (in about 1 km).

18.1 km. The end of the road — the light-house. The **light-house** is, generally speaking, not open to visitors. However, those who go out of season may find the light-house keeper far from unhappy to break his solitude with a bit of a chat and to show them the inside of the light-house.

After the eruption of the volcano, which sent the greater part of Strongyle to the bottom of the sea, the island sank into myth! And that myth travelled through time, taking on so many new names that its original traces were lost. Other myths intersected with it or arose from it, such, perhaps, as that of the existence and destruction of Atlantis. So, today, one does not know what name to give these eighty four square kilometres of land which disappeared below the surface of the Aegean with crash leard at the ends of the earth ...

YELLOW PAGES: GENERAL AND PRACTICAL INFORMATION

Note: every effort has been made to ensure that the information provided is accurate. However, errors or omissions may have crept in, and will generally be the result of changes occurring since publication.

1. GENERAL

- Area of Santorini: 75 km^2.
- Circumference: 36 miles.
- Distance from Piraeus: 128 miles.
- Longest distances by road: Oia - Akrotiri (lighthouse): 30 km, Fira - Oia: 12 km, Fira - Perissa: 14 km, Fira - Akrotiri (lighthouse): 18 km.
- Population: 7,328 (1981 census). Density: 98 persons/sq. km.
- Long-distance telephone dialling code: 0286.
- Post Office code number: 847 00.

Santorini is administratively part of the Thera province of the Prefecture of the Cyclades. The province also includes the islands of Amorgos, Anafi, Donousa, Irakleia, Ios, Koufonisia and Schinousa.

Administrative sub-division: into 14 communes: Thera (Fira), Akrotiri, Vothonas, Vourvoulos, Emboreio, Exo Gonia, Episkopi Gonia, Imerovigli, Thirasia, Karterados, Megalochori, Messaria, Oia and Pyrgos.

- Emergency telephone numbers: Fira Health Centre: 22237
Emboreio Doctor's Surgery: 29222
Oia Doctor's Surgery: 71227
Pyrgos Doctor's Surgery: 31207
Fira Police: 22649

2. HOW TO GET TO SANTORINI

The best way to reach Santorini is the boat. That is the only way in which one can discover it gradually and give oneself up, willy-nilly, to its charms. Departures by sea are frequent — almost daily. The passenger and car ferries start from Piraeus. There are direct connections and also lines which link Santorini to other islands — Syros, Paros, Naxos, Milos, Ios, Anafi. These, however, vary from year to year. In the summer there are connections to Rhodes and Crete. Those who are really keen on sea travel can take the irregular services, which afford an opportunity to get a brief taste of very many Cyclades islands both before and after the call at Santorini.

There is also an air connection to Athens — twice a day, summer and winter. In the summer, there are additional flights between Santorini and other islands, and charters fly in directly from abroad. Travellers arriving by air are warned to expect something of a disappointment as they arrive, on looking at the landscape round the airport, which consists of identical, sandy, grey expanses reminiscent of the surface of the moon. Patience, though; the other side of the island is quite different!

Santorini is also a port of call for many cruise liners. Visitors arriving this way will have about half a day on the island.

3. ACCOMMODATION

Santorini has hotels large and small, inns, rooms for rent, camp sites and youth hostels. Information from travel agencies.

The large hotels, with or eithout swimming-pools, have, depending on their class, the same amenities to be found in hotels all over Greece. The smaller hotels tend to be more austere, cheap, built for those visitors who expect to spend most of the day outside, and who are concerned on their return only to shower and sleep. The rented rooms are more picturesque: in this way one gets a chance to live in a typical Santorini house and become acquainted with the people at close quarters. The last of these factors is not one to be overlooked.

4. TOWNS AND VILLAGES TO STAY IN

Apart from Fira, the island's capital, and Firostefani and Imerovigli, there are two other locations on the island which attract large numbers of visitors: first, Kamari, on the eastern back side of Santorini. This is a coastal village with a marvellous beach of black sand and all the delights of the seaside. Secondly, there is Apano Meria (Oia), a most northerly town, which is picturesque, majestic and wild. The sea can be reached easily from Oia, as well.

Naturally enough, accommodation is to be found everywhere in Santorini, in every village, at every beach, and not just in the places we have mentioned. Indeed when the tourist season is at is height there is a lot to be said for going straight to one of the smaller centres. It is far from unpleasant to be able to cut oneself off in a quiet and charming setting.

5. GETTING ABOUT

There are buses to all parts of the island. In addition, there are taxis and cars and mopeds to hire. Mesa Yialos can be reached by cable car. The way back up is much more fun by donkey, the traditional means of transport. Boats leave Mesa Yialos every day for trips to the volcano, Thirasia and even Apano Meria. The travel agencies organise bus tours to various parts of the island.

We have assumed, when writing the itineraries which form the second main part of this book, that the visitor has some means of transport at his disposal. There is, however, nothing to stop one doing them gradually, even on foot, and organising as one wishes the way in which one makes use of one's time on the island.

6. THINGS TO SEE AND PLACES TO GO

Minoan site:	the excavations at Akrotiri.
Hellenistic monuments:	the excavations at Mesa Vouno.
Christian monuments:	Episkopi Gonia, Prophet Elijah Monastery, St. Nicholas Nunnery, Catholic church of the Dominian nunnery (Fira).
Geological phenomena:	the volcano and caldera, the pozzolana quarries.
Museums:	Archaeological (Fira), Byzantine and Folk Art (Prophet Elijah Monastery), Naval (Oia).
Handicrafts:	carpet-weaving school (Fira).
Beauty spots:	Apano Meria (Oia), Skaros, Mesa Yialos.
Beaches:	Kamari, Perissa.

The information about the various cultural events held on the island each summer is easy to obtain on the spot.

7. SPORTS

The sport or recreation for which Santorini is most suitable is walking. A glance at the second part of this book will be enough to show that large parts of the itineraries described there are much more fun when done on foot. Some, indeed, can be done only on foot (the Volcano, the Theoskepasti church, the Prophet Elijah Monastery, Mesa Vouno). Anyone who wants to really get to know Santorini will do so in this way. The island is not really very big, anyway; though one must have the time, of course.

Naturally enough, the second major recreation is swimming, which is in any case the chief aim of most visitors. Our routes give details of the best beaches on the islands and also of what visitors should be careful of on some of them. Among other sports connected with the sea are wind-surfing, fishing and spear-fishing, all of which are perfectly possible in Santorini if one has the right equipment. For the very bold, there is even shark fishing in the caldera. Indeed there is a book, available on Santorini, which describes a local method of doing this. In all other respects, good luck to them.

Not all that many years ago, the locals would look forward to the beginning of September for the hunting season to start. Quail and turtle-doves were the chief quarry, given that Santorini is on their migration routes. However, over-hunting led to these birds becoming scarcer and scarcer, and eventually strict legislation was introduced to protect them. In view of this, anyone interested in hunting should apply to the police for information and a permit before hand.

Lastly, route 7 in this book (p. 113) notes the existence of a tennis court in Karterados.

8. NIGHT LIFE

Night life in Santorini is seasonal and is intended for visitors, especially the younger ones. Fira in particular buzzes with bars and discotheques in the summer. Santorini responded with great facility to the demands of this kind of entertainment, brought with them by the tourists, since there were available the spacious areas in and around the old cellars which were converted in the twinkling of an eye into attractive night life centres along western lines. And so today there are quite a number of bars with taped music, discos and other night spots.

The 'bouzouki', the instrument most closely associated with night life in Greece as portrayed in the cinema and elsewhere, took a long time to make its appearance in Santorini. There are, however, night clubs with bouzouki music today, and it is also possible to find clubs where Greek traditional dance and music can be seen and heard.

9. SHOPPING

The market in Santorini is reminiscent of all the parts of Greece where there are large numbers of tourists: there is an abundance of shops, one huddled next to the other, draped inside and out with clothes, souvenirs, handicrafts and other articles which tempt the passerby. It's not a bad idea to have a look inside: many of these shops contain merchandise which is both good in quality and cheap.

Apart from the souvenir shops, Santorini also has more specialised establishments: jewellers, antique shops, carpet shops and art shops. These, in particular, are interesting even if one has no intention of buying.

The jewellery to be found on Santorini is of exceptionally high quality — real works of art. The designs are original and so interesting as to be in demand from Athens and elsewhere, and there is a vast range of styles and prices.

The island's antique shops are a good place to look for the sort of souvenir which really makes a holiday unforgettable.

The works of Greek and foreign painters on display and sale at the art shops frequently take Santorini and its wild beauty as their subjects.

The carpet and rug shops contain work of original design and vigorous colour. Traditional patterns made up with the greatest of skill can also ordered and purchased from the carpet-weaving school run by the nuns.

Last —but certainly not least— are the island's own natural products. These may be cheapest souvenirs available, but they are often hard to find. The island's famous wine is the most easily available local product. There is a range of types: sparkling, bordeaux, 'nychteri' (a wine of superb taste —and deceptive strength— made by leaving the grapes overnight in the vat to crush themselves) and a sweet red 'communion wine'. Apart from the wine available straight from the barrel, bottled varieties are also sold and these can make an excellent gift. Among other local crops are the tomatoes (or tomato puree) and the island's peculiar little cucumbers. 'Fava', the chick-pea, for which Santorini is also noted, can sometimes be found on sale.

10. FOOD

There are more restaurants on Santorini every year, and of all types: the classic Greek cook-shops, selling mainly made-up dishes, tavernas with charcoal grills, Europeanised restaurants, pizza joints, kebab (souvlakia) shops and snack bars. Ouzo, Greek mixed salads and feta cheese are to be found everywhere.

What one has to really search for is the humble little eating-house in some village or half-deserted beach where there is a little old lady who has failed to adjust to the way things are today and continues to cook as if she were doing so for her own family. The taste of the food and the size of the helpings will more than repay the effort of searching. One should, of course, not omit to try the chick-peas (fava), the false meat balls, and the famous wine of Santorini (see pages 37, 38, 39). A little luck can put one on the track of the local sausage (especially in Pyrgos and Gonia) and of the very tasty white cheese known as *'chloro'*.

And one piece of advice: in restaurants, insist on the tomatoes in your salad being local ones.

11. LOCAL CUISINE

The cooking of Santorini does not differ much from that of the other islands in the Cyclades. 'Pseftokeftedes', however, are a very tasty traditional dish and are made from almost nothing at all. We give here recipes for them and for 'white olives', a Santorini sweetmeat which is in fact nothing more or less than sweetened almonds.

Pseftokeftedes: take 2-3 onions, 2 large tomatoes, mint, salt, pepper and flour.

Chop the onions up fine and grate the tomatoes. Mix with flour, salt, pepper, mint and half a glass of water to make a thickish paste or batter. Heat olive oil in a frying pan and, when hot, spoon in dollops of the batter to make a kind of small round pancake.

White olives: take 1/2 kilo of peeled almonds, 1/2 kilo castor sugar, 1/4 glass water and 1/4 glass orange-flower water.

Rub the almonds together with the sugar, water and orange-flower water and simmer until the liquid evaporates. Leave to cool, and then form into little balls. Sprinkle these with the castor sugar.

Format: 17 × 24 cm, Pages: 176
Fotographs: 150

THE GREEK COOKERY BOOK

You can visit culinary Greece through our last edition "THE GREEK COOKERY BOOK" that we prepared for you. In this book, you will find the representative greek dishes, traditional recipes and secialities for the official holidays with easy instructions to prepare them as well as numerous and rich illustrations and also the caloris corresponding to each dish.

BIBLIOGRAPHY

Note 1: The works quoted are in Greek unless otherwise stated.
Note 2: the articles cited in this bibliography contained in the book by M.A. DANEZIS **Santorini** (see below) are listed here with the indication DAN and the page number.

ΒΕΝΕΤΣΑΝΟΣ Δ.: *Η δράσις του συνεταιρισμού Μεσσαριάς*, in ΔΑΝ, σελ. 396.

BOULANGER R.: *Grèce*, έκδ. Hachette, συλλ. Les guides bleus, Παρίσι 1967, με συμπλήρωμα του 1970.

ΓΕΩΡΓΑΚΑΣ Δ.: *Τα ονόματα της ομάδας των νησιών της Σαντορίνης, Θήρα - Σαντορίνη - Θηρασιά - Καμένες - Ασπρονήσι - Φιρά*, in ΔΑΝ, σελ. 273.

ΓΕΩΡΓΑΛΑΣ Γ.: *Η γένεσις και η εξέλιξις του συμπλέγματος των ηφαιστειογενών νήσων της Σαντορίνης*, in ΔΑΝ, σελ. 19.

ΔΑΝΕΖΗΣ Μ.: *Σαντορίνη*, Αθήνα 1971. (Ο τόμος περιέχει πολύτιμα άρθρα και τεκμήρια που αφορούν τη Σαντορίνη. Από τα άρθρα αυτά, ιδιαίτερα χρήσιμα στάθηκαν όσα αναφέρονται αναλυτικά στη βιβλιογραφία).

ΚΑΛΟΚΑΙΡΙΝΟΣ Γ. +: *Η ιερά μονή Προφήτου Ηλιού του Θεσβίτου*, in ΔΑΝ, σελ. 145.

ΚΑΤΣΙΠΗΣ Φ.: *Τα αρχαιότερα κτήρια της Σαντορίνης ανευρέθησαν το 1866 στη Θηρασία και το 1867, 1870 στο Ακρωτήρι*, in ΔΑΝ, σελ. 83.

ΚΑΤΣΙΠΗΣ Φ.: *Οι ανασκαφές του βαρώνου Χίλλερ*, in ΔΑΝ, σελ. 55.

ΚΑΤΣΙΠΗΣ Φ.: *Τα καστέλια και η προστάτις των Αγία Θεοδοσία, βίγλες και γουλάδες, καταφύγια*, in ΔΑΝ, σελ. 121.

ΚΑΤΣΙΠΗΣ Φ.: *Η ονομασία Σαντορίνη*, in ΔΑΝ, σελ. 273

ΚΟΚΚΑΛΑΚΗΣ Ν. +: *Η εν Θήρα ιερά Μονή των Δομινικανίδων*, in ΔΑΝ, σελ. 167.

ΚΟΝΤΑΡΑΤΟΣ Α.: *Αναδρομή στην ιστορία της Σαντορίνης*, Αθήνα 1970.

ΚΟΝΤΑΡΑΤΟΣ Σ.: *Η λαϊκή αρχιτεκτονική της Σαντορίνης*, in ΔΑΝ, σελ. 221.

ΚΟΥΜΑΝΟΥΔΗΣ Ι.: *Τα λαϊκά σπίτια και οι εκκλησίες της Σαντορίνης*, in ΔΑΝ, σελ. 209.

ΛΟΜΒΡΑΝΟΣ Ι.: *Το κυνήγι του καρχαρία στη Σαντορίνη*, ?, 1982.

ΜΑΡΙΝΑΤΟΥ Ν.: *Σαντορίνη*, εκδ. Μαθιουλάκη, Αθήνα, 1977.

MARINATOS SP.: *Excavations at Thera - First Preliminary report (1967 season)*, εκδ. της Βιβλιοθήκης της εν Αθήναις Αρχαιολογικής Εταιρείας, Αθήνα 1968.

MARINATOS SP.: *Excavations at Thera II (1968 season)* εκδ. της Βιβλιοθήκης της εν Αθήναις Αρχαιολογικής Εταιρείας, Αθήνα 1969.

MARINATOS SP.: *Excavations at Thera III (1969 season)*, εκδ. της Βιβλιοθήκης της εν Αθήναις Αρχαιολογικής Εταιρείας, Αθήνα 1970.

MARINATOS SP.: *A Brief Guide to the Temporary Exhibition of the Antiquities of Thera*, εκδ. General Direction of Antiquities and Restoration, Αθήνα 1971.

MARINATOS SP.: *Some Words about the Legend of Atlantis*, β' έκδ., Αρχαιολογικό δελτίο Νο 12, Αθήνα 1971.

ΜΑΡΚΕΖΙΝΗΣ ΣΠ.: *Πολιτική ιστορία της νεωτέρας Ελλάδος*, 4 τόμοι, Πάπυρος, Αθήνα 1966.

ΜΗΝΔΡΙΝΟΣ Μ.: *Η ιερά πατριαρχική και σταυροπηγιακή μονή Αγίου Νικολάου Σαντορίνης. Παλαιά και νέα*, in ΔΑΝ, σελ. 161.

ΜΗΝΔΡΙΝΟΣ Ν.: *Δανέζειον οφθαλμιατρείον Θήρας, η «Αγία Βαρβάρα»*, in ΔΑΝ, σελ. 333.

ΝΤΟΥΜΑΣ Χ.: *Σαντορίνη*, έκδ. Δέλτα, Αθήνα 1979.

ΟΡΛΑΝΔΟΣ Α.: *Η 'Πισκοπή της Σαντορίνης (Παναγία της Γωνιάς)*, in ΔΑΝ, σελ. 149.

ΠΑΠΑΙΩΑΝΝΟΥ Ι. - ΣΚΟΥΡΟΓΙΑΝΝΗΣ Ι.: *Σαντορίνη*, εκδ. Βεν. Ησαΐας, Αθήνα 1977.

ΡΟΥΣΣΟΣ Μ.: *Σαντορίνη, έθιμα και παραδόσεις*, Αθήνα 1979.

ΡΟΥΣΣΟΣ Μ. *Σαντορίνη, το νησί της Φωτιάς*, β'έκδ., Αθήνα.

ΡΟΥΣΣΟΣ Μ.: *Μποριανοί τρατάρηδες*, in ΔΑΝ, σελ. 269.

ΣΙΜΟΠΟΥΛΟΣ Κ.: *Ξένοι ταξιδιώτες στην Ελλάδα*, 4 τόμοι, Αθήνα 1972-1975.

ΤΣΕΛΙΚΑΣ Α.: *Μαρτυρίες από τη Σαντορίνη (1573-1819)* = κατάλογος της έκθεσης ιστορικών εγγράφων στο Πνευματικό Κέντρο Μέγαρο Γκύζη, Αθήνα 1985.

ΤΣΙΤΟΥΡΑΣ Δ.: *Σαντορίνη, 15ος-19ος αιώνας*. Πνευματικόν Κέντρον Μέγαρον Γκύζη – Σαντορίνη. Αθήνα 1983.

ΦΙΛΙΠΠΙΔΗΣ Δ.: *Σαντορίνη*, έκδ. Μέλισσα, συλλ. Ελληνική παραδοσιακή αρχιτεκτονική, Αθήνα 1980.

— : *Νεώτερον Εγκυκλοπαιδικόν λεξικόν «Ηλίου»*, λήμμα Θήρα.

— : *Πραγματικός πληθυσμός της Ελλάδος κατά την απογραφή της 5ης Απριλίου 1981*, έκδ. της Εθνικής Στατιστικής Υπηρεσίας της Ελλάδος, Αθήνα 1982.

— : *The Reader's Digest Great World Atlas*, Λονδίνο, 1961.

The above works have been supplemented by many personal experiences and memories.

Index

SANTORINI HOTELS

Chora (Fira) (0286)

ATLANTIS	A′	22232
SANTORINI PALLAS	A′	22771
VILLA THEOXENIA (P)	A′	23386
VILLA RENOS (P)	B′	22369
ANTONIA	C′	22879
DEDALOS	C′	22834
ELLAS	C′	22782
EROLIA	C′	22155
KALLISTI THIRA	C′	22317
KAVALLARI	C′	22455
KING THIRAS	C′	22155
PANORAMA	C′	22481
PELEKAN	C′	23113
PORTO KARRA	C′	22979
SAN RAIZ	C′	23934
THEOXENIA	C′	22740
FLORA	D′	81524
LOUKAS	D′	22480
SANTORINI	D′	22593
TATAKI	D′	22389
ASSIMINA	E′	22034
KATRIS	E′	22584
KETI	E′	22324
LIGNOS	E′	23101
THIRASSIA	E′	22546
VINA	E′	22876

Kontochori (0286)

ANATOLI	D′	22307
LETA	D′	22540

Firostefani (0286)

AFRODITI	C′	22161
GALINI	C′	22095
KAFIERIS	C′	22189
GALINI B	E′	22095
MARGARITA	E′	22764
MYLOS	E′	22173
SOFIA	E′	22802
THIRA	E′	22863

Akrotiri (0286)

ADAMASTOS	B′	81188
AKROTIRI	C′	81375
GOULIELMOS	D′	81615
PARADISSOS	D′	81352

Emporio (0286)

ENEA MOUSSES	A′	81781
ARCHEA ELEFSINA	D′	81250

Imerovigli (0286)

KATERINA	E′	22708

Kamari (0286)

ATHINEA	B′	–
GLAROS	B′	–
ILIACHTIDA	B′	31394
RIVARI SANTORINI	B′	31687
ROUSSOS BEACH	B′	31255
ADONIS	C′	31956
AKIS	C′	31670
ALKYON	C′	31295
ARGO	C′	31374
ARTEMIS BEACH	C′	31198
ASTRO	C′	31366
AVRA	C′	31910
KAMARI	C′	31243
KASTELI	C′	31122
LEVANTE	C′	31160
MATINA	C′	31491
ORION	C′	31182
POSSIDON	C′	31698
TROPICAL BEACH	C′	31789
VATOS	C′	31660
VENUS	C′	31133
ZEFYROS	C′	31108
AKROPOL	D′	31012
ANDREAS	D′	31692
BLUE SEA	D′	31481
CHRYSSOS ILIOS	D′	31301
KARYDIS	D′	31474
NIKOLINA A	D′	31253
SIGALAS	D′	31260
TA KYMATA	D′	31694
TARELI	D′	31773
GIANNIS KAPELOS	E′	31166
DIONYSSIOS	E′	31310
NIKOLINA	E′	31253
NINA	E′	31697
PREKAMARIA	E′	31266
VILLA ELLI	E′	31705

Exo Gonia (0286)

MAKARIOS	C′	31375

Megalochori (0286)

VENTEMA	A′	81796
VILLA DOLFIN	A′	81663
SANTORINI STAR	C′	81198

Messaria (0286)

SANTORINI IMAG	A′	31874
PATINIOTIS SPYROS	B′	32332
ANNI	C′	31626
ARTEMIDOROS	C′	32281
KALMA	C′	31967
LOÏZOS	C′	31733
APOLLON	D′	31792

Karterado (0286)

NIKOLAS	B′	23912
ALBATROS	C′	23435
KATERADOS	C′	22489
LONTOS	C′	22146
BABIS	D′	22314
OLYMPIA	D′	22213
PALLADION	D′	22583
GIANNIS	E′	22552
NIKOS	E′	23737
TZINA	E′	22834

Vothona (0286)

CHORIO DAMIA	A′	32532
MARKISSIA	B′	31583
MENTITERANIAN	B′	31167
KALISPERIS	C′	31832

Oia (0286)

PERIVOLAS (P)	A′	71308
LAOUNTA (P)	B′	71204
ANEMOMYLOS	D′	71410
FREGATA	D′	71221
ANEMONES	E′	71220

Perissa (0286)

SANTA BARBARA	A′	21534
AMARYLLIS (P)	B′	81682
BLACK SANTI BEACH	B′	81773
ELEN	C′	81627
THIRA MARE	C′	81114
CHRISTINA	D′	–
MARIANNA	D′	81286
SANTA IRINI	D′	81226
TZORTZIS	D′	81104
BOUBIS	E′	81203
CHRYSSI AMMOS	E′	81109
MAROUSSIANA	E′	81124
MELTEMI	E′	81246
NOTA	E′	81209
PERISSA	E′	81105
RENA	E′	81316

Pyrgos (0286)

ZORBAS	C′	31433

Finikia (0286)

FINIKIA	C′	71373

CAMPING

SANTORINI (Fira)	22944
KAMARI	31453
KANTERA VIEW	81010
PERISSA	81343

To help you find
your way round Santorini
step by step, we also publish the most detailed map
of the island. It contains a town plan, useful information, a list of
hotels and a brief descriptive text.

Format: 17 × 24 cm, Pages: 176
Photographs: 180

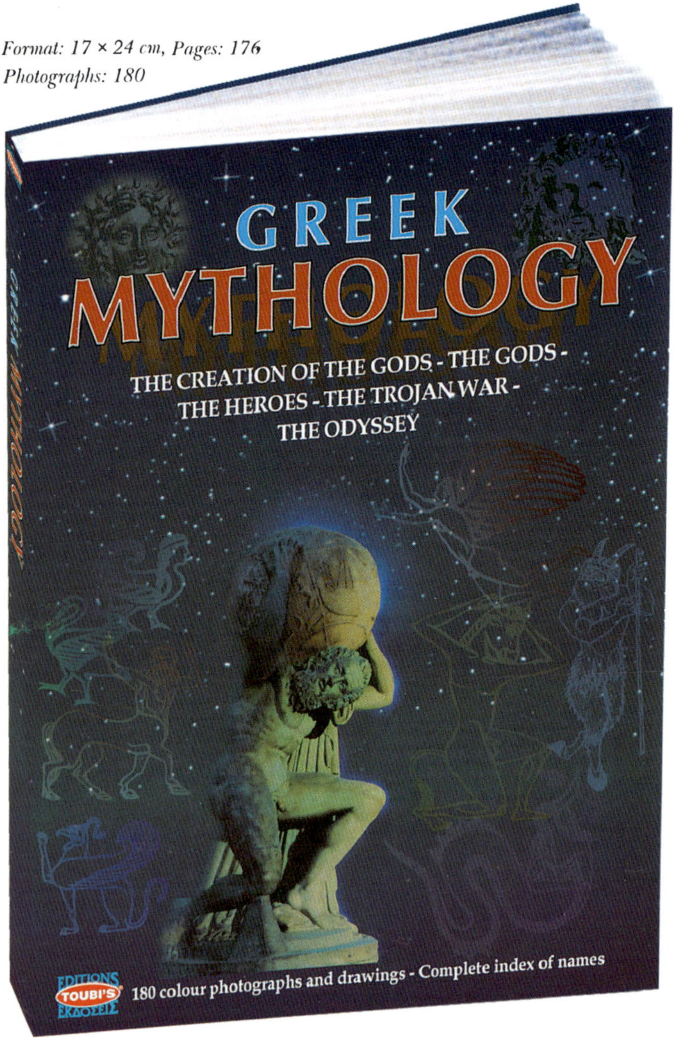

GREEK MYTHOLOGY

This special edition has been designed to present the main Greek myths. A work of considerable scope, written in a simple and expressive language, it is accompanied by 180 photographs and excerpts from ancient Greek literature.